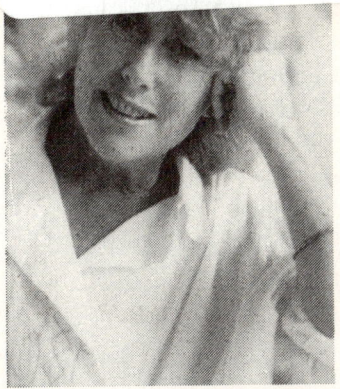

Gael Knepfer studied at Sydney University, and worked as a journalist in Sydney. She spent thirteen years in the United States, where she wrote for American magazines, radio and television.

In Australia, she divides her time between northern New South Wales and Sydney, where her work is largely devoted to Australian social issues. Gael is also the author of *Sex in Australia* and *Nursing for Life*.

Nothing truly valuable arises from ambition or from a mere sense of duty—it arises rather from Love and Devotion towards men and towards objective things.

Einstein

I, the captain of a Legion of Rome, have learned and pondered this truth; that there are in life but two things—Love and Power and none can have both.

Inscribed on a rock in North Africa

PLAYING IT BY THEIR OWN RULES

GAEL KNEPFER

Photographs by Colin Beard

HUTCHINSON AUSTRALIA

Hutchinson Australia
an imprint of
Random Century Australia Pty Ltd
20 Alfred Street, Milsons Point NSW 2061

Sydney Melbourne London
Auckland Johannesburg
and agencies throughout the world

First published 1990

Text copyright © Gael Knepfer, 1990
Photographs copyright © Colin Beard, 1990

All rights reserved. No part of this publication
may be reproduced, stored in a retrieval system,
or transmitted in any form or by any means,
electronic, mechanical, photocopying, recording
or otherwise, without the prior written permission of the
Publisher.

National Library of Australia
Cataloguing-in-Publication Data

Knepfer, Gael.
  Women of power.

  ISBN 0 09 169531 7.

  1. Women in the mass media industry –
  Australia – Biography. I. Beard, Colin.
  II. Title.

302.230922

Typeset in 11½/12 (condensed to 10½) Goudy Old Style
by Midland Typesetters, Maryborough, Victoria
Printed by Australian Print Group
Production by Vantage Graphics, Sydney

CONTENTS

Acknowledgements	vii
Foreword	ix
The Notion of Power	1
Cherie Romaro	15
Hilary McPhee and Diana Gribble	41
Jane Singleton	75
Ita Buttrose	99
Caroline Jones	121
Jana Wendt	143

DEDICATION

This book is dedicated to Clarice Bradbury whose love is her power, whose power is her love, and whose lunch is her lunch.

ACKNOWLEDGEMENTS

To my family with love.

Special thanks to:
Matthew Kelly: for giving me the idea for this book and for publishing it;
Jennie Dell: for her discipline in first draft editing and typing;
Margaret Connolly: Australia's youngest literary agent and no doubt the most nurturing and inspiring;
Jamie Grant: editor and poet who refined and healed this text;
Judy Major: whose laughter and typing run through the fabric of the book;
Colin Beard: indefatigable photographer whose camera finds the truth in each instance;
Wendy McCarthy: for her insight and for writing the foreword.

In appreciation of those who offered loving support and guided me into further understanding of the ego and the soul:
Dr Rob Simons; Annie Wayland Simons; Jan Dawkins; Katherine and Peter Arnold; John and Colleen Pathlander; Susan Yorke; Frances Plummer and the corporate wisdom of One Voice.

My thanks to the following people who helped in preparing these profiles:
Phillip Adams; Wendy Bacon; F. Bear; Helen Caldicott; Father Paul Coleman; Kevin Collins; Clint Dawkins; Adrienne Dodd; Helen Garner; Stephen Godley; Lorrae Graham; David Hill; Sue Hines; Kim Hoggard; Patsy Hollis; Sue Jobson; Brian Johns; Margaret Jones; Vicky Jones; Frankie Lightfoot; Craig McGregor; Jeff McMullen; Bradley March; Chris Masters; George Moore; Adam Muir; Barnie Muir; Paul Murphy; Lyn

Norbury; Geoff Rushton; Bob Scott; Pat Shepherd; Jodie Sherlaw; Gerald Stone; Carolyn Taylor; John Timlin; Dimity Torbett; Brendan Ward; Sue Ward; Don Watson and Dianne Willman.

To the seven Women of Power for their accessibility, for their articulate clarity and for their trust.

FOREWORD

Gael Knepfer and I started preschool together. Although our lives have taken very different paths we have kept in touch for more than 40 years. In those years we have been wives, mothers, and both of us in different ways have worked in the media. Gael's media experiences started as a young woman when she was a cadet reporter and worked in radio. She was very much an urban child and led what I thought was a sophisticated media-centred life. By contrast I spent the first 20 years of my life in the bush. My significant experiences with media were as a listener to ABC Radio for the four years I attended a one-teacher bush school.

In the following 20 years Gael lived away from cities and wrote books about sex and health, and I spent my life in cities learning to manage the media and writing books and articles about sex and women.

Our lives have again coincided with an interest in the media and women. When Gael first talked to me about this book she was fascinated with the relationship between media, women and power. My perspective was perhaps a little different. As a director of the ABC my observations were that women exerted very little power in the media until recently. I recall the years in the 70s when we were trying so hard to change the definition of women in Australian society, how we longed to hear women reading the news and being authoritative and strong on television. We wanted to see women in positions of confidence and stature managing media organisations.

This book reveals that in the last 20 years many of those objectives have been achieved. Everywhere we hear women's voices, we see women's faces, and slowly we are beginning to see women running not only their own media businesses but having positions of power and responsibility in large media organisations.

The women whose profiles Gael has written have been wonderfully honest with her. It is one of the great joys of the book. All of us will be able to recognise the experiences, the incidents, the moments of truth, for indeed they are universal themes. It is just that in this instance they are played in a media workshop.

For years I have been fascinated by the emotional energies women put in to balancing their private and professional lives. This book provides some wonderful insights into how seven successful and powerful women do that.

Wendy McCarthy
Deputy Chairperson
ABC 1983–

THE NOTION OF POWER

The power possessed by top people in top jobs is contained within, like air in a pressurised chamber. When its door opens, a draught escapes, and any person entering or facing 'the power' is slightly slowed in their tracks, becoming measured, often losing familiarity with the self, their balance upset, the scales tipped by the draught's powerful presence.

In this era, we are constantly referring to power. The word is used in advertisements: one I saw was for a certain 'hotel of power', where people of power put their powerful heads on the powerful pillows at night. Suddenly, we're nonchalant about 'power dressing', shoulder pads, restaurants, gold bankcards, designer luggage. What is power? Is it money? Is it charm?

The notion of power grew into something like a big beach ball with bright and varied spherical sections as I bandied it around in my mind. It passed across the desk, between the legs of chairs, and bounced off the walls. I grasped at it tentatively.

No-one wants to talk about it. It kept slipping away, elusive as an eel. In my mind one metaphor tumbled upon another in my efforts to describe its effect and its origins. My way of rescuing myself from this multifariousness was to design a template—a pattern or guide—which allows the ego and the soul to fit in an equal balance. The soul, the creative force, tempers the ego and helps bring about that balance, or alignment. I used this template in my journey to explore the essence behind the power of seven women in the media.

Do women in the media carry the same weight of power as women in merchant banking?

Who is the female Alan Bond?

Does Brian Toohey wield power when he executes cut'n'thrust journalism?

Is Chris Masters powerful because he unearthed what was to become the Fitzgerald Inquiry? He doesn't view himself as powerful. He says that when he learns of another hatchet-job on Jane Singleton, his first thought is: 'There but for the grace of God go I.'

Helen Caldicott, as a minder for the planet, is a powerful extension of the female family nurturer.

Ita's battle with Kerry, Rupert and Warwick is a power struggle with its own share of anguish. Her bright face emblazoning AIDS consciousness on huge slabs of cardboard dangling from the ceilings of Woolworths was always a bit unsettling. For the rows of women queuing behind trolleys, Ita represented their country's choice of inspiration and influence: a powerful woman.

Wendy McCarthy, deputy chair of the ABC, stands firm in her shoes, talks straight, and has been doing her homework since she was an eleven-year-old kid in the bush. She feels entitled to power. She thinks that people call her powerful because she is not exploitable. Seldom a week goes by when she doesn't agonise over the exercising of her power.

The media, in reflecting us back to ourselves, leads, shapes and models, and powerful media women reflect and further define the shape of our social consciousness. The seven women profiled in this book have been public figures in Australia's media history for close to 20 years in most cases. Each of them has the elusive quality of a star. Each woman has an appeal that is wide and multi-levelled, that impacts upon people vertically and horizontally. Each woman knows that her life as a contributor to this country's culture is not a sprint, it's a marathon. The image of more than one of these women has become engraved in the minds of most Australians.

The influence of Jana Wendt, the youngest at 33, was underlined recently when two teenagers who had been lost for days in bushland claimed when they were rescued that one of the fantasies that had kept them going was the hope that Jana Wendt would interview them on television. That is benign and public power.

Who are our heroines? Lisa Curry? Kylie Minogue? Politician Dawn Fraser, who is still on the tips of our tongues although her moment of glory was back in 1956? Germaine Greer? If there are any current public heroines, it seems that they're from the media, alongside the rock stars, film stars and sporting stars.

Cherie Romaro, media star, the top executive co-running 2DayFM music radio station, said: 'Well, I want to be in your book because I know it would give my parents pleasure to know I was being acknowledged for all my hard work, AND I don't feel at all like a woman of power.'

Ita Buttrose, who could whistle up the Prime Minister to launch her *Ita* magazine, when I asked for her to be photographed with her labrador on the sofa, said: 'Oh, that isn't the way a woman of power should be seen.'

To my request to see her to explore the issue of power, Jana Wendt said: 'Oh, I don't think I have any real power, I'm more like an island.'

Hilary McPhee and Diana Gribble were matter-of-fact.

There was comfort for them in having each other when asked to present themselves and their publishing house. They eased smoothly into talk of love and to the significance of their partnership.

Caroline Jones feels personally empowered as she falls in love with God. She is enjoying the resurrection of her spirit and knows it helps her with power struggles at the ABC.

Jane Singleton was grieving, and retrieving her self-esteem and her career. She was truthful and intimate about her loss. Her intellect gives her a power that her temperament baulks at.

These people became 'my women' as I clamped on my own shoulder pads, stashed my tape recorder in my bag, and set off to sample the draughts of power: phone around, keep the energy up, follow referrals, get the gate pass, choose a well-cut jacket, talk to top boys and girls in swivel chairs, speak of power or don't speak of it—test the water.

'Of course, you know there's a war of hatred between the sexes, don't you?' said *60 Minutes* reporter Jeff McMullen.

Yvonne Preston writes about Retrogressive Feminism.

Adele Horin writes: 'In Australia, Equality is a Dying Myth'.

The nerves tighten. Suddenly the power issue, which had been like a tossable beach ball, is more like metres and metres of snarled fishing net, tangled and knotted, full of barnacles, dead fish, jewels, shells, seaweed, cans, watches, lightbulbs, driftwood, glass, wallets, sinkers, floaters, cans, pearls, all coiled and furled into an indecipherable mound, rolled and dumped against the sea wall of a bleak and trammelled city beach. Waves hit it, shoving it harder against the beach. Dwellers walk past it, kick it, read about it, lose sleep over it, bite bits off it, bask in it, give it to someone else, weep over it. John Laws might hire a crane to shift a bit of it; he might tease out the portion he wants and take it home. Cherie Romaro might retangle his teased-out section and pry into another part. She passes it on. We watch.

Then I wonder whether levels of power can be gauged by

levels of protection: to 'get' to Jane Singleton took numerous phone calls in which a non-communicative secretary kept forgetting who I was and where I was 'from'. We set a time, presumably blessed by Jane. Reception announced me by phone. Twenty minutes later a woman of the slightest build emerged: 'We have no record of your appointment, please wait.'

Twenty minutes, to watch the receptionist eat, drink, smile, talk, shuffle.

'Miss Singleton will see you anyway.'

Phew!

There she is in the corner of her office, looking drained after three hours on air, and in the midst of a program post-mortem, which comprises hefty ego-wrestling among the team of females. The room is shot with tension. Power in a radio cubby-hole; power with the wobbles? Jane seemed to bite through the ego games, exuding a passion for dissecting the content of the program.

' . . . and Gael, what do you think the purpose of all this [waves hands], the purpose of life is?'

Boom.

'Serenity, ultimately.'

'Serenity?' she says scoffingly. 'That's bullshit.'

I like her. She had already intuited that I want more from her, and she was scared to confront it. She's more transparent than she knows. I catch the beach ball smoothly, empowered by understanding.

I felt pretty powerful as I raced up some side stairs next door to Capricorn Publishing, and ended up in Ita's private foyer with its new formaldehyde-laden carpet. I announced myself on time. The Ita look-alike secretary minced into an open doored, adjoining room: 'Gael Knepfer? How did she get up here?'

She made no effort at styling her voice: 'She's early. Tell her to wait.' Street voice. Tough.

She had grabbed the beach ball, hard against her bosom. Power as the possession of control. This was to be our first meeting in 26 years, since we were cadets together on the *Daily Telegraph*. She held the power, having gained it by the edge of accusation in her voice. Twenty minutes passed. Slowly the disempowered feeling faded. I felt familiar with myself again, and interested in how Ita operates.

She was holding the power of control down to the most minute detail. Suddenly I saw her as a little girl programmed to make no error, nor to have one occur through oversight. Her choice of greeting, her use of familiarities and colloquialism were, in the same instant, second nature and full of calculation.

My sense of ease seeped back into my bones as I distanced myself from her performance and acknowledged her genuine, infectious warmth.

Later, at the Nine Network, I took the circuitous route through its labyrinths to the television goddess. Jana Wendt began by telling me: 'I'd prefer it if you didn't speak to anyone else about me. They don't know me anyway.' Yet this reserve diminished as I came to know her. She strode, lean and leggy, towards me in cavalry twill pants, remarkably young, straightforward and super-professional.

She has a steely etiquette. Her husband, Brendan, had told her of a good restaurant. A taxi was waiting. We cruised the shopping block and couldn't find the place: 'I'll jump out and find it!' She is nimble.

I wondered how the shoppers felt when they saw Jana running up and down the street.

I held the beach ball and sat quietly as the taxi followed this enthusiastic girl along the sidewalk.

Jana ordered saki and tit bits. We drank quickly and laughed. The ball passed between us easily. I switched on the tape recorder. She was funny, very funny, relaxed, disarmingly beautiful. A blend of flirty and flinty. I thought to check the tape machine. It had recorded nothing. The ball fell under the table! In at least 700 interviews the machine had never failed. Is Jana a witch? I wondered. This lissom, playful girl who loves food and drink and good talk; she had the multi-faceted beach ball resting softly in her lap.

THE NOTION OF POWER

When power passes easily between people, is there less ego involved? Is it that then two people feel an equal sense of personal power, as they bounce off each other, not striving to outwit or out-distance? Is it then that each person's soul is aligned with the ego, creating that straight, clean place within? As our relationships developed, it seemed that in each setting, each woman, including myself, was dealing with a power which fluctuated between exercising control and acting from the sense of personal empowerment which comes from such an alignment.

To sustain my momentum there were phone calls, referrals, doors opening, people in media setting limits and happy to talk within parameters.

It meant holding the beach ball tight and keeping my level of control-power at its optimum as I ran, head on, into personalities dwelling on Jeff McMullen's war of hatred between the sexes, into devastation as people are flayed and fired. Helen Caldicott told me about the Glass Ceiling: this is a level of top management, essentially male, above which women seldom rise.

At the time of Wendy McCarthy's appointment to the ABC, women were in the lower ranks of the organisation. In the top 100 key executive positions there were only two women: one a market researcher and one a lawyer. Margaret Throsby had her own program and Jane Singleton and Geraldine Doogue were reading the news. They were presenters and artists rather than policy makers and organisation shapers.

Some say it's a wise woman in management who concedes to men in the management of power because they are good at it. They have practised it; they have access to the system. They are the ones who have defined it.

Many of the men aged 45-plus are finding that their familiar support systems are disappearing, as their wives go to work and insist upon equal distribution of responsibilities and finances in the family. Yet these women, when they do make it into management, seem not to have developed their own private and domestic support structures because these things cost money.

The single woman still speaks of a perceived stigma on 'spinsters'. So no matter how cosy she may be with her lover in bed, the stigma of singlehood is still directed towards her. A similar prejudice extends to the working mother. Women may have secretarial support. In some cases they may have emotional support from men; but they don't have overall social approval for occupying positions of power. This is borne out by the pattern of overseas travel where, traditionally, men could take their wives along. There has been little provision for women to take their male spouses on business trips.

Conversely, men suffer from the stereotype that they are all competitive and go-getting. To be a person of public power carries with it responsibility. As Lord Acton said, 'Power corrupts and absolute power corrupts absolutely'.

As society changes more men are evolving as loving beings who need a world which has loosened up opportunities for them to have unusual positions in the community: jobs in which they could express their softness. That will remain well-nigh impossible while children are still reading books that indicate that Dad makes all the decisions in the family, rather than suggesting that all is well if 'Dad works for a girl.'

A male-dominated system of public power has kept women from sharing that power—and even pretended to them that rocking the cradle meant that they ruled the world. This is nonsense in the light of the way public power is organised in society. In terms of real power in the world today, it is accurate. Relationships between people, and people's relationships with themselves, are what is truly powerful.

Power and control, and the subliminal undercurrent of the war between the sexes, were difficult concepts to approach; more difficult still were integrity and love. My original definition for power was 'ball crushing'. Now, if asked, I'd say power can be another expression of love.

True power is love for the self. The sense of well-being and fulfilment we gain from self-love arises when the drive for success is aligned with the spiritual element within us all.

THE NOTION OF POWER

Jeremy Griffith in his book *Reconciliation* says: 'The truth is that the old, egotistical world where we had to live off self-aggrandisement and self-satisfaction is now spent. We are faced with complete exhaustion, i.e. global devastation, physical impoverishment of humans on a massive scale and everywhere so-called "spiritual emergencies" and a lack of cultural support which has led to total psychological breakdown. The old ways hold little appeal. There is great hunger for a new world, where we subtract rather than add to earth's problems.'

My files were growing plump with transcripts. The details were extensive. I had traversed the city in zigzags to people who shed light on media, women, power, and on the stresses and pressures on the people behind the entertainment industry—the system that helps to create our social consciousness. There was plenty of material with an emphasis on power of the dog-eat-dog variety. Below the surface lay the tenderness of each woman's truth. There lay the poignancy of success, that rested always with results, the insistence of the drive to keep going and the relentlessness of the treadmill.

My energy was lacklustre as I transcribed details of ratings, money, privileges, prices, pick-me-ups, workouts, prayer, death threats, singleparenting, miscarriage, divorce, loneliness. I saw rooms of cigarette smoke, demanding car phones, cruelty between colleagues, alcohol, stalking schizophrenics, hate letters, serial migraine, exhaustion, bulimia, decisions, alcohol, deadlines, exhaustion, vitamins, exhaustion. There was power all right; it was needed to keep up the pace. It felt as though we were under the siege of unrelenting panic, speed, decision-making, urgency and addiction.

Through my growing bond with the seven women I began to absorb the pace of their urban lives.

In agreeing to write the book, I felt charged with power, consisting of a fairly bold ego heightened by the recent publication of my previous book. I was pushing from a similar place within myself as was each woman. I had then continued to inflate my ego so that I would always feel larger than the purpose, driving myself to open doors, creating credibility for what was only a potential book and giving that book shape and substance with each introduction. I was trying to form relationships that attempted to cut through to levels of truth with each person.

I mustered the ego power to take up the challenge.

I didn't feel empowered as I worked. I began to see that personal power is related to fulfilment.

I was still plugging away at the typewriter, but wanting to fall asleep four times a day! I went to the G.P.: 'Gael, do you know the book is hitting you between the eyes? It's forcing you to confront your own power. Your own truth about what you're doing'.

Tears and an inability to think. I was determined to go on.

So what did I think about power now? Did it lie in my ego's need to inflate itself enough to meet the challenge? Was I operating simply from the power of control?

The urgency in my life and in those around me made me very tense. The general mood was one of speed, distraction and bewilderment, interspersed with shows of courage, force and determination.

I pushed away the feelings of exhaustion and doubt with more wine, more phone calls, longer and faster swimming lengths.

How satisfied or fulfilled were the seven media women? They go to work every day. Ita sees her magazine on the stands and then she goes home and pats the labrador. Is there then 70 per cent satisfaction in looking at the magazine and 30 per cent fulfilment patting the labrador? Would her life be any different if she was truly fulfilled?

Is Cherie fulfilled? She races against the clock keeping a steady flow of adrenalin rushing through the veins of the network, yet, 'having babies', she says, 'is the most wonderful career a woman can have.'

Jane said she ignored what we called her 'inner knowing' when it told her to stay with the ABC after she was fired from *The 7.30 Report*. She went across to 2GB anyway. In ignoring her 'inner knowing' she gave away her personal power. Is her satisfaction 60 per cent doing battle with the media machine? Is fulfilment for Jane the 40 per cent she spends playing with her children on the verandah?

One morning I left home at the crack of dawn to avoid the traffic. My interview schedule was Ita, Phillip Adams and Jana. It was grey and raining. There was only one other vehicle on the stretch of inner city road, a huge semi-trailer which hit my car, forced it into a post and concertinaed the back and front, totalling the car. I sat behind the wheel, rocked by the impact and noise and unhurt. My thoughts reverberated around the crushed car: 'What is really happening here? I must be supposed to get a message.'

I remembered Diana Gribble talking about her job as a publisher and of her bouts of overwhelming exhaustion and doubt: 'It takes nerve to go on and it takes nerve to give up.' She continued to publish.

Was she driven by ego and the power of control?

Had she then achieved some internal balance?

Lethargy took over me again: 'Gael, you're giving yourself glandular fever,' said the G.P. 'I'll give you B and C drips each day and try to beat it.'

How many people out there are having vitamin drips on the quiet? How many people are doing battle with the debilitating, delusional, addictive side of their ego? I was losing the sense of personal power which comes from being in one's essence, as I sank further into living with power only as ego and control.

There was nothing new in this version of power. The colours of the beach ball had faded.

Here were seven remarkable Australian women leading public and constructive lives, women of power as a consequence of the results they produce, measured in business acumen, money, style, influence and the impact of each personality. I could see that their lives were not constructed solely around ego and control.

I had to think further.

The emotional turmoil for public women in the late 80s and the quandary of whether women can find fulfilment in positions of public success and power was becoming clear to me. It seemed that the sense of power that comes from satisfaction in the work-place is different from the real power that comes with fulfilment.

Fulfilment, in other words, can be experienced at different levels, and the deepest level involves the soul. This is the level I am talking about when I refer to the power of love.

I took three months off and moved to my beach house in the country. The book had become a shield. A smokescreen for myself. It made for reactions that went 'Oh, power? Oh boy . . . ', and clever conversations would ensue. My ego was massaged by these exchanges. I could reassure myself: 'Well, you're writing a book, you can feel o.k. about yourself . . . '— yet I felt no power in this. It seemed I was disconnected from my soul.

It was a different matter when I got up at five in the morning, put on bathers and sloppy joe, got on my bike and headed for the beach as quickly as possible, pushing my bike hard over the dune. There, framed by the arched trees of the heath, was the exquisite eastern morning. A cluster of wetsuited boys, straddling boards, watched the sun inch its way into full bloom on the horizon.

I shoved the bike through the dry sand, hit the hard wet of a low tide and started to pedal. This month of August it is usually against a strong, cold wind, and it's wonderful. One day I said: 'O.k. this is it, from now on, no hands— the full length of the beach.' THAT feels powerful. It's tough on the thighs. It takes concentration when you're new at it, breathing hard and using all your strength.

In those moments I didn't need the book. I didn't need a shield.

There was sweat running down my back, though the front of me was cold. There was a biting wind in my teary eyes, through which I could see the beauty of it all.

THE NOTION OF POWER

The sense of personal power is a sense of internal balance; a balance between ego and soul. Neither is dominant. Each is serving the other. In this state of being in one's essence we will always make choices that are in our best interests, but we don't always trust ourselves with that.

Being in one's essence, I came to see, was like riding a bike, no hands, along a beach. The ego, in this analogy, is an unpredictable gust of wind, or a big wave, which upsets both your bike and the balance of your soul. Yet, unlike the wind, the ego can be devious and relentless.

The wave can assume many forms—it can be greed, or envy, or self-doubt—but once you have fallen off the bike a sequence of defensive behaviour ensues in which the self is lost. You become falsely animated; you might attempt to justify your fall with fabrications; you might even try to flirt with the concerned passer-by who saw you fall, in order to gain some control.

That's a way of seeing what goes on each day for most of us, as the ego looks for ways to take us out of our essence, away from the balanced inner knowing that is its greatest threat.

Each of the seven women, when asked to tell of a time when she felt fantastic, would mention a situation in which she was expressing love, and recall the accompanying sense of personal power. They spoke of giving birth or of making an effortless speech. They didn't speak of 'Oh, when I won at the races,' or 'seeing myself on a magazine cover'. I think of English writer and philosopher Iris Murdoch who says: 'Lack of self knowledge is a form of self sabotage'. She also said: 'There are enormous resources in the soul.'

Still, most of us continue to be self-conscious and cynical when there is talk of spiritual matters of the soul or the inner person.

Cherie, Jane, Hilary, Diana, Ita, Caroline and Jana are all beautiful women. They are original, courageous, intriguing and significant.

Each has been prepared to stand up to being scrutinised, analysed and embraced; each has been willing to be understood as a person and in turn to understand a more workable way of viewing the nature of power. Each woman had the confidence in herself to trust in the interview process.

Their integrity in this book comes through in their willingness to deal in the truth; to let others speak for and about them, and to allow their stories to be put through my filter system.

That truth is an expression of the power of their love— a love without control; an energy rather than a fixed reality.

Cherie Romaro

'GRAB THAT BATON AND RUN'

Cherie Romaro's story will always include the constant, and almost cable-like, link that she has with her large, close-knit family. Her attachment runs through the texture of her world at the top of Australia's radio industry, and transcends the distance between Cherie, in Sydney, and her family, in Perth.

Cherie is an Executive Director for the Austereo group of radio stations, a position to which she was appointed after seven years as Program Director for 2DayFM in Sydney. A major force in Sydney radio, 2DayFM was the last independently owned radio station in Australia, until it became part of the Austereo group in mid-1989.

'That's my Mum and Dad', she said, as she lit up and squinted through the first saltpetre blast of a tailormade cigarette at her crammed office notice board, an arm's length from her chair.

'The love between them is very special. We were all brought up in that love, and it's a part of us. That's one of my Dad when he was young'—she pointed to a handsome young man in his twenties—'My Dad's the image of Spencer Tracy. I can't think of anything else he's like. He believes in honesty, and truth, and working hard and reaping the rewards. Whenever I have a difficult decision to make I ask my Dad. He gives me my moral courage. My Mum, ah, my Mum. She's the creative one. My Mum has given me the flair, the sparkle, the "go-for-it". My Mum is a wonderful writer. I get my creativity and spontaneity from my Mum.'

Cherie unpinned three more photographs. 'These are my brothers; there's my sister Julie—she's my best friend—and this is my other brother. These are the people who keep me going'. She patted the photographs softly, and put them back in their places on the board.

On the wall behind Cherie was a framed gold record: 'Presented to Cherie Romaro by CBS Records in appreciation of your outstanding support of Sade's "Diamond Life" in Australia, December 1984'. Next to it was the Collector's Edition of *Whispering Jack*: 'Presented to Cherie Romaro for her outstanding support of John Farnham's "Whispering Jack". The Whisper Started Here, 1987'.

The identity of 2DayFM is that of Sydney's best music mix—the best of the 60s, 70s and 80s in music. The image is of a quality contemporary station for 35- to 45-year-olds. Its attitude is: 'Hey, life's great, do you remember this record?' The ambience is one of laid-back pleasure, with intelligent decisions as its backbone. It is said that if you listen carefully to a radio station you can sense the personality of the program director. From the person behind the reception desk, you can judge the feelings within the organisation. Whatever is going on inside the station will eventually come out of the speakers. If the music director is fighting with the general manager, or the news man is at loggerheads with someone that is what will emerge. It's what 'goes up the stick', as radio people say, referring to the transmitter aerial, that the audience hears, and the listener detects every time.

What was 'going up the stick' at the time of our interview, was evidence of Cherie's performance in her job as Program Director. Since then her arrow of ambition has shot higher up the professional scale, to Assistant General Manager and the executive position with Austereo. When we met, her desk was surrounded by ways of plugging in to music, with a cassette machine and reel-to-reel tape recorder close at hand. It was an office of sound, with record albums filed away beside videos and singles. Her diary was the only book. Cherie Romaro is an audio woman. If she had grown up as an American Indian she might have been named Music Woman or Woman of Song by her tribe.

Being with Cherie means you are surrounded by sound. With the station's broadcast a constant background presence, she likes to talk into the whole room when she's on the phone: 'Yes, mate, I know. I want an idea that sells new music, and an idea that sells old music'. Her hands free, she lit another cigarette.

'One phrase that I want to use is New Music, and the other one is 2DayFM Classic'.

She was looking into space, talking into space. The phone picked up her voice from the room and amplified her listener's voice back to her. 'It'll be going into one record: make that "Classics", 'cause I might do a sweep, so you can fiddle around and come up with some ideas'.

'You want modern?'

'Yes, modern, but not heavy, and very strong'.

'Almost dance music?' The voice filled the room.

'Whichever is the strongest jingle, that's the one I'll develop into a news theme, because the one we've got on air at the moment is not strong enough—we need to give it a new lease of life. If we get a strong jingle like the one on the TV commercial, I'd get you to develop a new theme for that. Must be full and rich. Have a fiddle, come back with some demos, and we'll have a listen. You broke again, dahl? Don't

come in with any trash, you've got a bit of competition. All right, sweet. Slow and sure, o.k. mate? Ta ta, dahl'.

Cherie's father, who went by the splendid name Sidney Louis Washington Edwards, was a fitter and turner in a timber yard in a small West Australian mill town. When she was fifteen, her parents sold up and moved to Perth for the education of their children.

'We weren't very well off, but we didn't lack for love. There wasn't enough money for the girls' schooling; preference was given to the boys in those days,' she said. Despite this lack of money, Cherie had been taught piano from a very early age and continued her rigorous music training as a classical pianist, even though she left school at 15.

'At 15, I was only mediocre, and I knew that I'd never be brilliant at it. If I couldn't be the best, I didn't want to do it'.

She taught piano at night and weekends for two years after leaving school, and worked as a casual in a record store. She was 'always desperate to get into radio'. One day, one of her applications yielded a phone call inviting her to an interview. She was there in fifteen minutes flat.

'Can you type?' they asked.

'Yes', she said, figuring she'd learn fast.

'Well, here's a typing test'.

'Oh, well', replied Cherie, 'I get very nervous. Could you leave me alone?'

She remembers a glamorous secretary with a big topaz ring watching her peck away with two fingers.

'Are you very, very nervous?' asked the woman.

'Oh yes, very', said a determined Cherie.

She was called back into the manager's office and he said: 'Well, we know your typing's not much good, but you seem like a bright young lass. We'll give you a shot'.

Cherie was given a job in the record library at 6PR. Her parents were concerned: 'But women don't succeed in radio; you'll be poor . . . '

'That became my driving force', Cherie said as she leaned

against her executive desk, mercurial blue eyes catching the light. 'I vowed then and there that I'd make it; I'd run the full distance. I don't want to do anything that I'm not going to be best at. I chose a career that I thought I could be best at, and kept it up.'

Cherie watched, listened, and learned. Within a year, when the Music Director left, she was moved into his slot, with the promise of becoming Program Director if the ratings soared. They did. It's more than twenty years since Cherie became Australia's first female Program Director, at the age of 18.

She cut her professional teeth in a male industry, at a time of great scepticism towards females, who often were paid only half as much as their male counterparts. Cherie pushed uphill all the way, driven by her burning desire for perfection. At first, she was nurtured by her parents, and guided by her then boyfriend, Terry Romaro, who says: 'I've always known that Cherie is a star'.

Cherie worked for 6PR until she thought that management would never move her on. When she felt the time was right for a change, she took off for 3UZ in Melbourne. This was followed by a stint on air on the Gold Coast. Then Perth's 6PR had a change of ownership and format, and Cherie was asked to return as Music Director for their 'Beautiful Music' programming. She accepted, went home to Perth, and married Terry Romaro. Twenty-five years on, Terry retains a deep love for, and insight into, Cherie, even though their marriage was destined to break up under the strain of their diverging commitments.

While she was working in Perth, yet another phone call came to change Cherie's personal and professional destiny. 2SM in its heyday of the 70s in Sydney invited Cherie to be their Music Director. 'This is it', she said to herself. Sad to leave Terry and her family, she said to them: 'I'll only do it for a little while, and then I'll come home and settle down'.

'Terry and I flew back and forth to each other', Cherie said. 'He was always with me, whether he was in Sydney or not'. The separation did not last long. Cherie was gathering

CHERIE ROMARO

know-how, and loyal staff who would come with her along the way. The next change came when Rod Muir offered her the opportunity to return a second time to Perth, to be Program Director for a down-and-out radio station, 6IX, that needed revamping.

'Yes', she said. 'Smaller market', and she returned, much to Terry's delight. The press described her as the 'Hatchet Lady From the East'. She started hiring and firing, wielding her now-developed brand of power.

Her next move was to accept Rod Muir's offer to start his newly licensed FM station, 2MMM in Sydney. 'Oh, Terry, I wanna do that', she said; and he said, as he had before, 'Great—it'll be good for you'. They parted again.

Cherie walked into the bare shell of MMM and became part of the team who designed the concept and station jingle that still exists. After three years, dissatisfied with the job, she left. 'After I walked out of MMM, I was sitting at home on my own, thinking "My God, what have I done? I've dashed

a dream!", when the phone rang. It was Willessee's 2DayFM—
"Would you like to direct our new program?" '

George Moore, whom Cherie calls her most valued and professional announcer, met Cherie 15 years ago when he was doing the night shift on 2SM: 'She was never pushy, but a little brash in her early twenties; she was trying to get ahead', he said. '2SM was the number one station in those days, competitive and aggressive, and nowhere near the feelings of friendship and camaraderie that exist in here. And that's a lot to do with Cherie'. George had just emerged from his morning hours in the studio.

'In radio, program directors come and go at an incredible rate. The average life of a program director is eighteen months, and for an announcer on a major shift, maybe two years', George said. We were sitting opposite each other at the long, narrow, antique refectory table that had been chosen by Caroline Laws in the early days of the station, when it was owned by John Laws, Mike Willessee, and Graham Kennedy.

'I rate Cherie as the best program director I have ever worked with'. George was probably remembering the twelve that came and went during his fifteen-year acquaintance with Cherie—a rapid turnover rate which impacts on everyone at a radio station, not just the program directors themselves.

George said: 'There are a lot of ego games and head trips in this industry, and the way Cherie works is to acknowledge ability and experience, and to build a mutual respect'.

Cherie is more comfortable thinking about her soul than thinking about her ego. In the privacy of her soul she knows what it is to reflect back on the day's work and think: 'I could be a better person if I did that. Why didn't I do that?'

'I've always been taught that a healthy ego is good, it's part of your pride; but then it was drummed into me, forget about your personal ego and what you achieve for yourself, think only about what the team will achieve. And that seemed to be more comfortable for me. I feel comfortable as part of a team', she said.

But ego—what Cherie calls 'pride'—is not without its

importance to her: 'It's a pride thing that every day I achieve something on a business level—communicating with people is a big part of that. The key thing is pride, and communication comes second; and dealing with people on an everyday basis, and the relationship that builds with them, which drives me continually to achieve and succeed . . . '

'Is there fulfilment in that, Cherie?'

'Yes! Of course—95 per cent of the time. I am happy doing it, and while I'm happy I still want to do it—but that doesn't mean that I don't want to add to it'.

At the time of our interview, Cherie was just days away from being married for the second time. She had settled into her new position as Assistant Manager of 2DayFM under the umbrella of the Austereo organisation, and was experiencing great relief with the calmer waters ahead since the change in her position. Even having a baby had become a possibility.

'I'm ready for this next step, this commitment of marriage now, whereas before I couldn't think about that', she said. 'This job is more responsibility, but less pressure. Now I feel clear enough about my own life.

'But it's not enough for me just to be at home and have a baby. It makes me happy to work this hard. I have to have goals; my goal has always been to help make it successful with the team around me'.

One-time producer of Channel 9's *Wide World of Sport*, David Hill, observed of Cherie that we tend to overlook resourceful, hands-on, nuts-and-bolts human beings like her. 'The media is not a commune, it's a dictatorship', he said. 'You've got to stamp your own personality and what you want on the program, because if you don't like it, as producer and director, the chance of anyone else liking it is fairly remote. Behind any successful programming will be found a fairly dictator-like person, who says: "That's what I want, and I don't want that."

'Power is influence. If you have power you have influence, and if you have influence, you have power. Someone like Cherie never mentions the words power and influence, because she's got it. She knows she's keeping her audience . . . ' David

Hill scooted his chair across the carpet, and hit the dial of his sleek sound system. It blared forcefully, lyrically, into his office. ' . . . because she's decided that at seven minutes past ten, Paul McCartney will be on the radio.'

Cherie has an uncanny ability to tap into the psyche of a metropolis. She knows how to satisfy that mass psyche. She has influenced an enormous listening population, a high percentage of them with significant disposable incomes. She sees to it that these people are made to feel good. That's the bottom line. Radio and television set out to make people feel good. They are extensions of the travelling players of the Renaissance, storytellers who are keyed by intuition and gut feeling.

'Every song, every record means something different, and brings back special memories, in the minds of every person', said Cherie. She was wearing tailored black pants and jacket, and a white, up-to-the-neck silk blouse. Diamond bows dangled around her ears. 'Music says everything. It brings people together, happy, sad, warm, bitter. It has messages, lyrically, socially, politically. It satisfies'.

2DayFM is profitable because Cherie and her team choose music that unerringly hits the spot for an affluent segment of Sydney and environs, who in turn are influenced to buy what the team at the radio station chooses to advertise. With that reputation, the station commands a powerful place with advertisers and entertainment entrepreneurs.

Cherie has woven around herself a team of inspired and committed people. They provide a backbone for her expertise; and many of the young ones make up the ongoing apprenticeship program that is an integral part of 2DayFM. Many young people struggle to get even a foot in the door of radio. Those with the media gleam in their eye often have to pack themselves off to an outback radio station, resign themselves to three or four notices, and try to sell the local café a schedule on air.

It is important for an apprentice-oriented station to have a universal policy of training up their employees, looking after them and keeping them. Cherie has created this 'tribal' group around her by the power of a very loving nature, blended with an extraordinary drive for perfection and success. Training this group of young people is a pivotal point of Cherie's contribution to the world of radio. Herself a consummate professional, she is determined to pass her own high standards on to the next generation of announcers, music directors, and program managers.

By her love she, in turn, empowers people to perform to their utmost. By her stringent work ethic and example of discipline and determination, she causes these people to want to do their best. First they may do their best in order to gain her approval; but along the way they find that by extending themselves they can feel good, even great!

Power in radio is what comes out of those speakers. Radio is about people and attitudes. The on-air person has to perform and sound cheerful every day, and it's hard if there's been a fight at home, or a problem with management, for that person to let go of a negative frame of mind. Radio communication is a two-way thing. Human emotions are involved in the putting together and sending out of the radio program; and on the other side, there are the human emotions of those receiving the signals. To put these two forces together is to create a volatile situation. Yet once you've been in it, it's very hard to get out of it. It's like an adrenalin drip.

'Maybe she's a nurturer because she's a woman—and yet our managing director Bob is a nurturer,' said George Moore thoughtfully. This was at the time when Cherie was still program manager at 2DayFM.

'Bob cares about how the staff feels. That's good business practice', George went on. 'Of course, I'm aware that Cherie is a woman. I'm aware that she wears perfume—none of the other program directors wear perfume! But we don't think of her as a woman when she's talking professionally. She may even have her make-up out on the desk and be putting on her lipstick, but she remains at that point Cherie Romaro, program director. At a table at night with her man, she's Cherie, woman. And she isn't an example of women in radio, or an ad for women in radio; she's an ad for Cherie Romaro.'

'Jodie', called Cherie to her secretary at her desk, on the other side of the wall outside Cherie's office door. Two expectant young musicians were there, offering a tape for a jingle.

Jodie, a bit like a compact and spirited little filly, moves in through the door as one does in tight skirt and high heels. She is wearing a black T-shirt with shoulder pads, with a 'New York' patch over her left breast, floating among tiny red stars. She's one of the Fabergé, Kaepa, Reebok girls: black stockings, deep voice, streaked hair, eyes flashing, sexy legs.

'How about a cup of coffee for our guests?' Cherie suggests. They decline.

'Then I'd love one—and a cigarette', Cherie keeps her end up.

Cherie tries to control her smoking by not carrying a packet of cigarettes. The girls bring her one at a time and leave it near the lighter on her desk. The musicians sit opposite Cherie as she concentrates on the ritual of lighting her cigarette. 'Peter and I used to work in a wedding reception band', says the female musician with her high heels tucked under her chair.

Cherie pays careful attention to the girl's introduction to the music they are offering to 2DayFM: the couple has a new jingle for the station and they want Cherie to like it. 'Let's have a listen.' Cherie swings her chair around to her reel-to-reel machine and laughs throatily. The sound of 2DayFM comes across with voice harmony and backing: 'Two-Day-Eff-Em with More Non-Stop Music Today Until One!'

They all beat their feet.

The girl leans forward to point something out. Cherie interrupts: 'Oh, yes, I can hear. The change in the melody is not quite as strong . . . ' She closes her eyes and taps into herself. She smokes, and concentrates.

'These have to have longevity; they have to have the ability to go on a higher rotation that any other song. But over a period of two years, each time someone listens they must be able to hear something else'.

Cherie carries with her the luxury of the feeling of

excitement; the possibility that something brand new could happen at any moment.

'It's got merit—it comes close', she tells the waiting pair. 'I'd like to refurbish the old 2DayFM jingle. The melody's fine. I want someone to play around with it, give it a bit of bite. It needs that dirty sax essence, y'know what I mean?' She stops the jingle tape and switches her sound system over to the radio station. 'A screaming sax and instrumental. *Terms of Endearment* stuff'.

She is radiant. Her earrings bob. They sit forward towards each other. She animates and draws them into her plan, lighting her third cigarette.

'I'd like to play your jingle to my assistant, get his reaction. Mine is that it comes very close, but it doesn't kick arse. Maybe it needs an instrumental break in the middle. It usually takes me a couple of weeks to work it all out'.

Her station is still playing. She punches a phone line out to the studio. 'Just turn your level down a bit', she tells the on-air announcer. She doesn't miss a trick.

Turning back to the musicians: 'The good thing is, the timing's perfect. I'm a musician myself, and I know what I want. I have to try to tell that to the musicians and the producer. You're talking about a full-on music track that's gotta be the quality of a Billy Joel album. That's the only way to go. So it comes in beautiful and strong as "Just The Way You Are". That's what I want. I would spend as much on a jingle as if I was making a full-scale album. We get the best people, and if I thought your voice was the one, then that would be it. O.k. Nice to meet you. Leave it with me'.

When they had left, Cherie said quietly: 'Ten times a month I turn people back. I know what I need. Not a wimpy jingle following Elton John. Sixteen grand later, we've got a piece . . . '

'Whenever I have a difficult decision to make, important to me and to the station, I phone my Dad', said Cherie. 'He basically says: "Well, if you really don't want to go along with them, then fight it all the way, even if you have to walk away from your job". With his advice, I have never laid down when I believed in something'.

Cherie added that her ex-husband, Terry Romaro, has also always been there for her, guiding her through the labyrinth of her career. Professionally he has been her strongest influence, even though he's not in the media business—he runs a shipping agency in Perth. Theirs was a relationship of two people bound by a strong love, being pulled by commitments in opposite directions. It was a strenuous road for them both, fraught with personal anguish and heartbreak, as they conducted their long-distance marriage. Now she's married to David, a decision that took some time for her to make. She could only make it confidently after her promotion from program manager to assistant general manager at 2DayFM, with responsibility both for the managerial and the creative sides of the business.

This time she's prepared even to consider motherhood in addition to her work. There's a subliminal corporate message purveyed to women in the media, that they cannot hope to be a major influence with a high position in the organisation if they are going to have a family. The message is that it's not o.k. to opt out of corporate management for a couple of years to be there for the baby—yet why not? Women are beginning to question these limitations and in all the professions are getting bolder with their opinion that of course they can raise a family and be totally professional in their careers.

Interestingly, it is now more common for a man's curriculum vitae to list among other pursuits the fact that they are 'raising two children' or whatever. Wives and mothers have always been able to exercise a certain amount of power in families; more and more it is being recognised that that sort of power—love tempered with common sense—can be transferred with great benefit to the professions.

But there is still envy among media women for people like Jana Wendt, who managed to fit having a baby into the midst of a glamorous, highly paid job.

CHERIE ROMARO

Cherie was smoking another cigarette. She sipped a Diet Coke. Her voice was strong, but sounded chipped, as she dictated a letter to Jodie, who takes shorthand with maroon finger nails darting across the page, stilettos crossed under the chair, wearing black-rimmed glasses.

'You ain't nothing but a hound dog!' swells as background sound in the office, and beyond the door where the female staff sashay across the carpeted floor: music fills their work world. They move their bodies, sing softly, tap rhythm.

Smoke drifted from Cherie's ashtray as she dictated answers to today's stack of listeners' letters, smoothing them out flat in their new blue folder. The phone rings frequently as the ash builds on the end of the ongoing cigarettes.

Radio is an immediate business. Comparatively few letters get written in the course of a week. It seems that by the time the ink has dried on the paper, the matter is over and it's on to the next problem.

It's a world of excitement and risk-taking, combined with the heady complication that radio people tend to live on their nerves because of ratings surveys. Four times a year, people's jobs are on the line. That has enormous implications for families, wives and children. The stress levels take their toll. The positive force is that radio work is a real buzz, and that buzz never stops.

Radio makes reports on things as they happen. There isn't the time lapse of camera crew, processing, and then on-air. Radio is the 'hot' medium, according to media guru Marshall McLuhan. It tells people about *now*, and it seems that the demand for this element is increasing. People read the papers the next day for fuller explanations but our attention absorbs less and less as speed and stress levels increasingly rule our lives.

Music radio is an opiate. It calms down the frenzy of the everyday lifestyle while at the same time filtering the news as cleverly as possible. After 22 years Cherie's temperament has become attuned to this demand. Stayers like her become accustomed to problems and demands coming left, right and centre, every hour of the day.

'It's not running the race that's important to me', said Cherie. 'It's whether you get the gold medal or come fourth. The pay-off for running, for me, is the self-satisfaction in achieving something, and if I can walk out of here every day and say, "Well, I've achieved something!", I get great satisfaction. This industry is so cut-throat. It's here one day and gone the next. For me to be able to survive is a great achievement in itself; but I don't want just to survive—I want to win. That keeps me running'.

At the station one is constantly reminded of this fact: that Cherie being a woman doesn't come into the evaluation of her work performance. At 2DayFM the days of anything being based on whether one is male or female seem long gone; it's whether you can do the job, and whether you make it work. There are women reading the news, selling radio, announcing, managing, and directing.

Sadly, it's from the listeners—and the female listeners at that—that direct resentment flows towards on-air women. There seems to be some fearsome hatred out there in suburbia, regularly directed at female talent. The reasons for this remain a mystery. Maybe those women at home unconsciously compare themselves and their lives to a perception of an up-market female media performer, which stirs up enormous resentment at their own lot in life and makes them confront their isolation with self-criticism. Maybe.

2DayFM employs 43 people and 60 per cent are female. The word around the traps is that these females do a better job. They pay more attention to detail, and are capable of anticipating needs ahead of time.

Cherie was having a meeting in the long, narrow, airy room of the music library, where the essential music trinity of library, computer, and filing system is housed.

For this meeting, Cherie's voice became smoky, efficient, desultory—like a 'star'. The bare bones of the station—the choice of music sequence—was in the hands of the people in the room. Cherie shared a Diet Coke with big Brad, her 28-year-old assistant: 'One of the leading creative people in radio', she said definitively. Gerry, the red-haired music and computers mastermind, was there, and Susie, Cherie's quiet, understated, un-made-up young protégée, who had the job of researcher and librarian. She had started at 17 in the same way that Cherie had started her career. Susie believes that Cherie employed her because she is calm. Cherie confirmed this: 'That calmness gives her a head start. She will be one of the greats, believe me'.

'What about "Satisfuckshun"?' Cherie laughed, as they kicked around their insights into the Mick Jagger concert the night before. What comes out of these combined minds at each music meeting is the secret of the station's success. This combination of heads mutters, listens, throws in an idea here and there, hums, gazes into each other's eyes, listening again, getting specific. They sang softly; they referred to their opposition. A sunlit gum tree showed through the stripes of the venetian blinds behind the tableau. Posters of Stevie Winwood, 'Back in the High Life'; Sting, 'Nothing Like the Sun'; Sade, 'Stranger Than Pride'; INXS, 'Kick', all beamed down on the quartet. The cigarette lighter was passed around; blasts of the initial drag furled towards the ceiling. The Diet Coke went around again. The unit seemed to strengthen; an hour passed in no time at all. 'Don't Worry, Be Happy'.

'That's a hit', said Cherie with certainty. 'It's got it'. She was unlikely to be disputed, and of course she was absolutely right.

Brad whistled in a lazy and accurately tuneful way. It may not even have been the song that was playing at the time. He was constantly throwing song snippets into the room, a hum in mid-sentence, a riff for punctuation. Suddenly, on the TV set fixed to the wall that everyone had unconsciously been keeping an eye on, Debbie Flintoff-King won her Olympic Gold Medal in the 400 metres hurdles by a nose and a chest. It seemed to symbolise the energy in the room, as well.

The music sequence for every minute of every day is selected from the station's 'universe' of music. That universe, and the selection for each segment of the day, is done by a combination of technology and native instinct. It can no longer be done by intuition alone, as Cherie would have done it in earlier days. The selection must now be a blend of gut feeling with the hard facts of research—elements that have only come into prominence in the past decade. Cherie retains her reputation as the one program director in Australia who still insists on including the 'feel' of the music as a valid element in selection.

'It's the difference in our philosophies', said Brad. 'In our jobs we are trying to judge what people will like. We all have gut feel, but at that point it's incredibly difficult to be objective, because you are really looking at the music subjectively. You can make judgments through experience, but you need research to back it up'.

That's the difference between Brad and Cherie historically. The younger professionals have grown up with computer terminals and surveys, and the marriage of the two is an important ingredient at 2DayFM.

The station's 'universe of music' consists of 1200 records—basically anything pre-1989—selected by chart successes and research. There are a further 1000 tracks that can be drawn upon for particular segments, like classic hours or special weekends, and there are 1500 tracks on rotation. There are ten different rotation categories, varying from once every six hours, to once every five, six or ten days, as well as tracks that might be played only a few times a year for special occasions. These categories are formulated by the quartet who met in the library, and the computer spits it out according to what it's programmed to do.

Garry spends time going through each hour, track by track, and fine-tuning with the human touch. He and Brad spend at least four hours on the delicate operation of working over each day's music. They consider the sound of the records, the pace of the song, then the pace of each 15-minute segment. The tracks must flow, the era must be noted, the strength of the 60s and 70s music added so that there will be variety and balance, colour and interest, enough to capture the pulse of the metropolis.

Cherie trained Brad as a junior five years before. He was

on midnight-to-dawn shifts, and she trained him up and shifted him through the ranks to become her assistant. Then he felt he should go out and try program directing on his own. A position came up in Melbourne and Cherie thought he was ready to do it.

'He has tremendous talent', said Cherie. 'But they didn't know how to handle him. He needs for the person he's working for to have faith in him, to let him make his own decisions. In twelve months his confidence had gone, so I put his replacement back on air and invited him back as my assistant for another couple of years'. Brad is talented, volatile, and doesn't accept second best. Cherie admires and loves this young man, and enjoys his creativity in the studio. 'I can give him an idea and he can produce exactly what I want; he reads me beautifully', she said. 'I admire the fact that he has been prepared to come back and work with me until the right opportunity comes'.

Most of the staff at 2DayFM are very young, even though they are dealing with an adult format. Cherie would like to employ people with less obvious talents, start them off in lower positions and develop them, so that if someone leaves, they can go on to the next step. Cherie believes in this internal development, where the experience is locked in to the station.

A young, leggy, bubbly girl came breezing in to 'touch base' with Cherie. She had been a sales secretary who had wanted to go on air, then eventually on to television. Within the station, after-hours, Cherie would put her through her paces, do airchecks, and make tapes, as she primed her for going on-air. Finally a spot became available in a country town. The girl sent her tape out and got the job. 'They all keep coming back', smiled Cherie with a whimsical expression. Then her mercurial face changed again. 'She might be good enough to come back to a city station one day. It might be 2DayFM'.

Brad acknowledges that Cherie has never held back in teaching him anything he wants to know—and he admits to wondering: 'Why would anyone tell me this? This is a major advantage that this person has over me, and there are only a limited number of jobs in this field'.

Cherie's response is that people with a good attitude should be encouraged; it's very important to her. She said that there are always a hundred people who have technical abilities, or who say the right things, but the attitude and the aptitude are rarely found in combination. 'I would never hold anything back from the young ones that I believe in', she said. 'They are our legacy, and essential to the future of radio'. It's a profoundly important aspect of her commitment.

'Cherie was always the one to defend someone in the firing line', said Terry Romaro. 'So many guys would not still be in radio if it wasn't for Cherie saying "Hang on, give him another couple of weeks". She's a bloody radio professional. She's lived and died radio, and it's played havoc with her personal life in the past. I take some blame for that, too', he said softly. 'I wish I'd used a bit of insistence somewhere down the track'.

His voice broke. There was silence on the long distance line from Perth. 'Maybe I could have curbed her sense of ambition; but she loves the excitement of the challenge. She's unaffected by all the bullshit. She's a real human being—a wonderfully refreshing change'.

Silence on the line. 'Sorry', he said, softly. 'I'm her greatest supporter. She's out there toughing it out for herself with a lot more pressure than we know, and it affects her physically as well. She is a star'.

Silence. 'When you've got something, it's not until it's not there that it cuts so deep'.

Cherie was quiet in her office, her blue eyes strong. 'There was one time when Terry really needed me, and I put my work first, without realising', she said. 'He wouldn't tell, and I didn't read it. He started to lean on another lady, and only then did I realise that I should have been there. I've learned a very good lesson. I blew the most precious thing in my life then, and now, in this new relationship, I won't do that again. I cherish this new love, where I am stable and happy and in the same city as my career. It's a real luxury for me. I no longer think that conquering the world is the be-all and end-all'.

It is in her work that Cherie invests her personal sense of identity and it's in her workplace that she emanates the love, concern, power and need that many workers manage to divide between home and work: so she is dependent on her job to return to her the sense of empowerment and fulfilment which other women might achieve in a successful relationship or as a mother.

It's this aspect of complete involvement that highlights the addictive quality of Cherie's professionalism. And all this could change. Cherie's October 1989 wedding was an indicator that her career was at a point where she could share herself between a man and her job: her marriage may well be the catalyst for healing her addictive involvement in her work.

One of the young announcers—a boy in boots with a beeper on his kangaroo-hide plaited belt—took his seat opposite his boss. He was restless in his chair.

'You're a slow learner', Cherie told him. 'I didn't want to growl at you yesterday, but you were reminded at each break to play the promo, and you kept forgetting. You just have to concentrate. It's a key point. You can't shift anything—not promos, not anything—and the reason is that the client gets a list of his exact times, and that is really strict'.

'I promise you it'll come good—and the more I'm hassled about it, the worse I'll be', he said, straightening from the waist.

'Well, I don't want to spring you, but the thing is, you were reminded at one break, and the next, and the next, and you finally did it on the fourth'. Cherie was breathing shallow, eyes firm. 'I was sitting there when it was happening, mate, and I just thought "PLAY it, mate, NOW—all you've got to do is press the button and play the promo—it shouldn't be tense, it's on the log, PRESSS!" I can't understand why it couldn't be done'.

He came back: 'It's like you're in a car and you put the blinkers on instead of the windscreen wiper'.

'But you've been driving here for three years, so I don't

take that', Cherie's body had also risen from the waist.

'Well—I'm sorry, and I understand. I'm trying to be more conscientious'.

'Just DO it!' Cherie still had more to say. 'Next thing, mate, is that we're going to drop all editorial. In your talk breaks, the first priorities have to be everything the station is doing, whether it's a number on the weekend coming up, or "Wasn't the Mick Jagger concert great?"—once you've got that locked away into your talk breaks, then you can do an editorial. I can give leeway once you've got your commitments to the station delivered on-air—then you can do your own thing, but every time you open your mouth I want enthusiasm about what the radio station is doing'.

This 25-year-old was trusting Cherie, who kept going: 'The main criticism is that they can't hear you. It gets to a point of aggravation. Your heart wasn't in it, and you could hear that—I sure could. Even when you've got negatives, you've gotta say "Well, I'm here to do the job and I'll do it to the best I can". Even if you don't agree'.

The phone rang. The caller was doing sums for Cherie on the other end of the line. The phone voice filled the room. Cherie concluded the call sharply and efficiently.

'You've gotta stop breathing while you're talking. Breathe out and push it out. You should say one line and bang! into your commercials, instead of struggling. Ten seconds is a liner. You have to do them, but you don't have to do a 30-second commercial'.

Cherie coughed as we listened to the young man's voice from the on-air tape; now his air-check. Her throat was irritated: she had smoked a lot, drunk very little, and had no food, and it was getting on for three in the afternoon. Thoroughly chastened, the young man took his leave.

The sun had started to glint through the aluminium blinds, filtering a pretty light, signalling the winding down of the working day for many folk. Cherie was not necessarily one of them. Some nights she works till 11 o'clock. Cherie won't put up with fools and she will fire someone if she has to. She gives everyone one chance, points out the problems, sends them away, and if they do it again, she's no longer tolerant.

'I don't like doing it, and I always say to myself that the day I enjoy firing somebody is the day I give up. As long as it's still hard, and as long as I feel dreadful when I walk out of this place having had to do that, then I feel I've still got some balance going'.

Cherie has had some intimidating phone calls after having fired people who blame her for the lows in their careers. 'Perfection is the only way to go', she said. 'I won't compromise because if anyone accepts anything less then I don't like working with them, because they're not striving. I can tolerate mistakes. Being in that studio for hours is like being in a little cocoon; the person in there has to be brought back to earth sometimes, and reminded that he's got a whole audience out there, listening. It's like inviting someone to dinner and not preparing a meal. These kids have got to have the right fortitude to go the distance. It's a race, it's competitive, it's fast. They have to have the right emotions to go with their ability. Enough to run the full leg of the relay without dropping the baton, otherwise they'll never get there. I'm a great believer in "Grab That Baton And Run!", despite all the obstacles that are put in your way. If someone falls over in front of you, jump over and keep running'.

'Let's go to my place', said Cherie. 'I don't feel like going to the gym any more. I can put on my tracksuit and we can have a little meal and play with the cat'.

She drove swiftly, of course. With one hand on the car phone, calling her Dad in Perth, she steered her way with the other, through the peak hour traffic, away from Sydney's city lights. Closer and closer to home, along soft Harbour roads with trees. 'Hello Pop, how are you? Is everything all right? Oh great, oh that's good. I'm so relieved. How are you feeling? So what time are you going up to the hospital? What happened when you rang the doctor? Oh, good, that's good, Pop. I'll ring Mum in the hospital tonight. If you don't answer I'll know you're still on your way. Love and miss you, Pop. Bye bye'.

'For me, I need it all', she said to me, watching the road. 'Happiness, joy, success, I'd like to have it all. If I'm not successful at what I do, I wouldn't have the self-respect and confidence that I need. When I go home, I won't be happy unless I feel good with myself. I need home, family, love, the highs and the lows, the career'.

She wound the car slowly around corners and along darker streets that ran down towards the water. 'I went downhill when I was going through my divorce. I'm a great believer in emotions causing health problems, and when the realisation hit me that there really was this divorce from Terry, a divorce I'd never dreamed would happen because all of our love was still there, then I got pneumonia and went down for five weeks. Didn't pick up for three months. My health goes in the low times; but I have good resilience'.

Cherie parked beside a reserve overlooking a twinkling piece of Harbour.

'I know that I can't take my desk and my station home with me, and that ultimately my happiness lies in family and the balance of love in my life'.

She gathered her satchel and papers, and climbed down narrow stairs where jasmine hung from rock cliffs. It was a perfumed evening, with crickets in the bushes and little boats, their lights gleaming, moving slowly below. She was at home, on her little verandah, with her pure white cat.

Cherie's house is soft inside. All white walls, with a delicate suspicion of blue; lacy curtains and cloths. The cat is thirteen years old. Cherie moved through her house with ease and speed.

'I left in such a rush this morning', she said, as she leaned down and picked up her morning towels, her gown, and pieces of the day's papers, as she led the way to her bedroom.

'This is my room'. She showed me a room of feminine beauty, white and blue and lacy. She folded and sorted, and slowly eased off her ice-blue silk suit, putting it aside for the dry cleaner, and pulled on a white track suit. She put her hair in a black ribbon and slipped on her black-rimmed glasses, ready now to pad around on her thick rugs and show me the nooks and crannies and memorabilia.

'I still believe that motherhood is the greatest career of all. I may work twelve hours a day, but at least I can come home, kick off my shoes and that's it. With a mother, it's 24 hours a day, seven days a week, and she has to organise everything. I look at Jana and think she is fantastic, doing what she does and still being able to have a child. I look at Maggie Thatcher and think she's an amazing woman, she's had the kids, she's done it all. I look at Dawn Fraser for whom I have tremendous admiration. She's had hardships, hard training, marriage breakdown, ups and downs—and a child'.

Cherie was making cool drinks, putting little bowls in the microwave, feeding the cat.

'I'm now a close protector of my private life. I've seen marriages go wrong for no reason. I'm in a new life now, and I want to protect this new love. I don't want this relationship to be vulnerable. Even though I know I feed off the pressure at work, when I walk in here I can switch off easily. David and I play sport, we ride our bikes, we take each other on at squash. He hates to lose as much as I do, so we're well matched. I'm so lucky to have been given a second chance'.

Cherie carried a speedy and delicious little feast to the low table in front of the sofa.

'I've seen other women have children; I'd like to think I could. I'm not so stupid as to think I wouldn't need help—a nanny seems to be the key. My Mum told me that babies don't have to change your life—you just get the baby to fit in with you! I don't want to wake up at 45 and think "Oh God, what have I not done?"—especially for me, with such a close-knit family upbringing. Even today with everything so happy in my life, I feel deprived of my day-to-day contact with my family'.

The tribal feeling at 2DayFM is no accident. Part of it stems from the clan-like love Cherie has for her world. She loves to watch her 'kids' as they come through, and to be part of their climb; and to know that when she is old, she will listen to the radio, and some of these young people will be at the top in their field, and she'll know how she played a part in that.

'Listen', said Cherie, 'when I get old, I want to sit down and listen to good radio, and I want these kids to give it to me'.

Hilary McPhee and Diana Gribble

'A PLACE OF OUR OWN'

The McPhee Gribble building is one that croons—'soft around the edges like a siren's song,' said John Timlin, the longtime occasional companion and lover of Diana—the Gribble of McPhee Gribble.

'How is it to be married to Hilary? I think it's impossible, quite frankly', said Don Watson, the living-in-his-own-residence husband of McPhee. An ironic glint in his expression showed he did not quite mean it.

'Don't forget that some authors say they would pay to be published by McPhee Gribble', quipped my agent, Margaret Connolly, before I set off to meet Hilary and Diana in Melbourne.

With plenty of tapes and an open mind, I spent my time in the plane thinking of what I might ask these two women who had founded the stylish, exciting publishing house which had a reputation as the best independent publishing organisation in Australia. They were women from whom other publishers stood slightly aback, treating them with respect.

'Who will be more approachable?' I wondered, staring out on to anonymous clouds. The anonymity of the sky was calming before my first meeting with Diana Gribble and Hilary McPhee. They were reputedly formidable women with feminist tendencies who sat on the boards of councils, examiners and judges of writers. In the Australian publishing industry they were forces to be reckoned with.

The double glass doors of the McPhee Gribble building swung open easily. The entrance foyer opened into a grand open space, airy, softly lit, with Japanese rice-paper blinds filtering the light. The work areas were marked by drawing tables and trestles. There were book stacks dividing the room. Off to the right, a group of people were sitting in a circle on a nest of comfortable black print sofas: six of the seven were women.

'Come in! You must be Gael!' Hilary was facing the door—attractive, sophisticated, throaty-voiced, welcoming. The six women turned towards me and smiled with curiosity. The low table, piled with colour, supported a bright blue coffee pot, chunky Italian cups and saucers, and a big platter of crusty bread, olives, antipasto, and slices of lean meat.

'We had a sumptuous office dinner last night. We all cooked Italian. Everyone in here cooks. We're a little hung-over. I'm Diana'. A relaxed and gracefully soft-bodied woman with a wonderful laugh extended her hand. Hilary and Diana had separated themselves as the dominant women in the group. These women, with their staff of eleven, turned out 50 of Australia's cleverest, most poetic, and most contemporary books each year.

One of the essential elements for success in publishing is to be in touch with contemporary society. There was a contemporaneousness in the McPhee Gribble booklist which instantly distinguished it from other houses' lists. Hilary and Diana are profoundly interested in the exploration and examination of the values of today; values that bring about change. These women have a reputation for 'staying on the edge', and they tend to surround themselves with like-minded people. They work with those people, and with those movements, rather than with those who are satisfied with the status quo and the cultural cringe.

'It just so happens that they are two females with an enormous and intuitive publishing instinct', said Brian Johns, managing director of SBS Television, and the man who had established a vital publishing relationship between McPhee Gribble and Penguin books when he had been director of the Publishing Division at Penguin. 'Helen Garner is very much their author', he said. 'She represents that contemporary quality. *Monkey Grip* has been an all-time success for McPhee Gribble. It set a reputation because ten years ago it seemed a very daring book to publish. *Puberty Blues* came shortly afterwards, and reinforced the McPhee Gribble reputation as risk-takers. Both books gave Hilary and Diana a bit of commercial gloss when they were made into successful movies, which positioned the fledgling company quickly and firmly'.

When McPhee Gribble first joined with Penguin, it seemed they had resolved the greatest problem faced by every small publisher in Australia, the problem of distribution. Until that time, their books had been delivered to booksellers by a succession of different wholesalers, from the 'alternative' styled Book People, who went bankrupt in the late 1970s, to the 'establishment' firm Angus and Robertson.

The company McPhee Gribble was founded officially in February 1975, though their first book was not published until 1976. They began with a novel which was to become an Australian classic, Glen Tomasetti's *Thoroughly Decent People*—Diana Gribble laughs as she recalls that it was a hardback priced at $6.95.

In November 1983 Hilary and Diana made the agreement with Brian Johns at Penguin whereby all publicity, marketing and distribution would be undertaken by the larger partner

WOMEN OF POWER

Hilary McPhee

in what was a co-publication arrangement, while McPhee Gribble were limited to an editorial function.

Brian's reasons for linking Penguin with McPhee Gribble were twofold. First, he had a desire for Penguin to become a strong originating publisher. By taking on the McPhee Gribble list, he would dilute Penguin's reputation as a simple paperback house: that is, as a publisher which concentrated on buying up paperback rights to books published elsewhere in hardback, rather than originating the books themselves. And second, he would be developing an Australian list— something he was doing already under the Penguin imprint. An Australian nationalist, he wanted to support a strongly indigenous publishing house, which is what McPhee Gribble had become.

Brian Johns was one of the men who had an influence on the development of ideas at McPhee Gribble; the man seated amongst the women when I first entered their building, Michael Langley, was another.

At the beginning of 1989, after Brian Johns had left Penguin to become the head of SBS, McPhee Gribble asserted their independence by severing the co-publication arrangement with Penguin. They maintained their association with Penguin as a distributor, but their books no longer carried the Penguin logo. As they had been in the 1970s, McPhee Gribble were once again an independent publisher.

The new relationship meant that Penguin could no longer affect the direction of the McPhee Gribble imprint. It is an imprint which has put a different complexion on the publishing of Australian literature, especially fiction, and a different complexion, too, on the business of taking our culture seriously.

Thoughts about their influence on our culture were running through my mind as introductions were made. The women intuited that the thing to do was to let me settle and feel my way; and for their own part, they were participating in a coffee-and-snacks ritual, discussing work-oriented topics, combining a design discussion with the domesticity of cups and saucers and titbits of food.

I thought about how it would be for any writer, coming

here and being welcomed into this big room, drawn into the circle, and exposed to these marketing, design, management, and editorial women.

I was to learn that the whole point of McPhee Gribble was to have as many people as possible feeding ideas into each other's projects. The open-plan, softly screened building was ideal for that overlap of ideas. Everyone was free to express opinions on work in progress, with no fear of getting into corporate trouble.

The design and quality of an executive's offices, and of the goods or services purveyed by that executive, are suggestive of the quality of power that emanates from him or her. Some executives exercise 'power over' their environment and staff: everything is functional and tense. Others share 'power with' their colleagues: their premises reflect more than one influence and the variety in the decor and in the untramelled personalities of the staff is refreshing.

Some express the power of their position indirectly, through manipulation—smiling men with bad reputations, whose staff have to walk on glass to stay in favour, never knowing where the line of accessibility is until they cross it. Some maintain power through the hard work of others while playing golf and banking fat salaries—they also maintain opulent offices and efficient, well-groomed staff because every detail increases their ego-preening glory.

People working from their ego-centre risk using their position of power to control others. When people are working from the essence of who they are, with their soul aligned with their ego, the power of love is in operation. This is easier to achieve for people who truly love what they do, and who have come to an agreement with themselves about how far they are going to let their egos get in the way of doing what they do.

Women tend generally to be more in touch with the pleasurable things in life, and more prepared to take some of those pleasures into the workplace—tasty things to eat, brewed coffee, a cushion on the chair, funny or touching pictures on the wall. On the whole men are more goal- and

success-oriented, and tend to forget those little humanising touches in their professional environments.

Hilary and Diana established McPhee Gribble at a fertile time in their lives. While the new company was starting to grow, Hilary was also creating a second family with a new husband, and Diana adopted her only child, Anna. They set up in the business in much the same way as they might set up a new home, but with the added skills and experience that they brought to their work, there was an underlying core of determined professionalism.

'We spent days choosing our coffee pot', laughed Diana. 'And we ran the business like a petty cash tin!' Essentially, what they were doing at that time was creating a 'place of their own', with a creche out the back for babies and a place to which older children could return after school.

Their attention to detail stood them in good stead. The constant driving force towards their development as entrepreneurs was the need constantly to generate new ideas in order to get themselves paid, so that they could uphold their domestic responsibilities and therefore justify the fact that they were no longer at home.

They worked out of a garage in the early days, budgeting stringently and paying themselves wages that fulfilled their domestic straight-down-the-middle split of financial responsibilities with their husbands of the time. They didn't need any capital investment, and yet, they point out, if they had been men, it would have been at this time that the bank manager, the accountant and the lawyers might have assumed that they would want to borrow half a million dollars to set themselves on course.

But they didn't take out a big loan, and were glad later to be free of the pressure it would have brought upon them.

Both women grew up in Melbourne. They knew each other slightly at Melbourne University, where Diana half-finished an architecture degree course and Hilary completed an arts degree. When they met later, both women were doing jobs they didn't like. They became close friends, and used to ponder ideas of what they might do together.

Hilary had been working in publishing. It was suggested to them that they produce a series of twenty children's books: the famed *Practical Puffin* series. It was to be the beginning of a fresh contemporary style. They researched and wrote the stories, and packaged the series, injecting into them a style beyond the ideas of the time.

With their advances and royalties, Diana and Hilary accepted a manuscript from a new writer—Tomasetti—and published her book. The first stone had been thrown into the pond and the ripples had begun.

They have remained entrepreneurial in their planning, their style, and their low-profile public relations. They were quietly competitive, and quite comfortable about it. They injected their own personalities into the organisation of McPhee Gribble, and developed around themselves a style, a symbolism, and a code of ethics which distinguished their benign hierarchy, with its relaxed accessibility, and made it very much a reflection of the values of the 70s. In keeping with the times, they were not on about head kicking, stark efficiency, number crunching or blind success-orientation. The success orientation of McPhee Gribble was and is tied in with how one lives one's life.

Yet Hilary and Diana are both attracted to tradition. They are big on Christmas, and certain old-fashioned ways of running their houses and raising their children. They are interested in the female line in their families, and want to hand down ways of living that they learned from their mothers and grandmothers.

'Our grandmothers are particularly important to us', said Diana. 'We somehow use their standards as a basis for our behaviour towards each other and towards the business. It is unconventional life pinned down in this very traditional way. On one level we have a non-hierarchical office and on the other it is very, very carefully structured. Other people wouldn't see this, but we know what we're doing and these ethics and ideals and little traditions that we hold so close become translated into the "style" of McPhee Gribble'.

Hilary and Diana have a vigilant interest in the stylishness of things—not in the easy-to-see, packaged, modern, graspable, substitutable, commodity-pungent, one-generational, long-socks-and-shorts, readable-label variety, but style in terms of content, durability, subtlety and familiarity with an 'on-the-turn edge to it. 'Sometimes it's as shabby as hell', said Hilary, leaning forward, trying to articulate what their style consisted of. I ventured a guess: 'Is it the way the floor in here is smooth and old and has tatty beautiful rugs on it, and eleven pairs of interesting, soft, comfortable flat shoes that tread and retread across it in a maze all day long?'

After sitting there quietly for a day, I had noticed the constant rhythm of McPhee Gribble; the soft padding sound of women moving around, tapping into each other's projects, assessing, talking, deciding, delving together in the high-ceilinged space. For me, the floor, the rugs, and the soft shoes symbolised the aliveness, naturalness and purposefulness of the place. It felt airy and Australian.

'Has it been hard to turn your lives upside down, divorce

WOMEN OF POWER

Diana Gribble

and blend families while still running and expanding McPhee Gribble?' I asked.

'I think that having the office was a saving grace!' Diana replied. 'It made it terribly easy in a way, because we could just come in the door and here was McPhee Gribble, a place of our own, and it was here every day'. She let out a big belly-laugh, seeming to express relief. 'We could always come in the door and there it was, and only at the end of the day did we go out through the door and face the chaos of our other life . . . '

'I can't imagine how women go through those dreadful domestic upheavals without something else in their lives', mused Hilary, who perhaps more than Diana has needed to use McPhee Gribble as a refuge from domestic disharmony—a place of her own where she has been able to have a sense of mastery over her day-to-day experience. It's a sense of success perhaps easier to achieve at work than at home for many talented women.

It is hard for a perfectionist business woman to maintain her work and keep her husband happy, integrating the workload of a huge project or a demanding job with a sexual, mature, romantic partnership. One of the ironies of life in the late twentieth century is that increasingly we come to require all those services that the aristocracy expected in the late nineteenth century: people to look after the house, gardeners, teachers to look after the children, babysitters, maids and domestics.

Many people would now love to live like the high Victorians, with at least some of those support services; some would say that running at the pace we do, it's impossible to manage without them and that there is a financial and psychic cost in 'getting by' in the dual role of business person and homemaker. It's a particular pitfall for powerful women who tend to want to do it all with the same excellence and attention to detail—satisfy their man, supervise their kids, and make headway in a world where it takes a bit more sparkle for a woman to be taken seriously than her male equivalent.

There's a feeling shared by many competent, professional

women that it's not o.k. to come home from the office and say to their mate: 'I'm stuffed, I'm stressed out, leave me alone'. They feel that as soon as they hit the deck at home they have to be perfect—as if to make up for having been out at work all day. Ambitious women tend to spread their ambition across the whole vista of their lives: they feel responsible for maintaining high standards in every area. So they tend never to say that they can't cope with kids or their husbands because they want to focus on their work; they would rather try to do both well, and often get seriously over-stressed as a result.

But for the woman who has no outside-the-home, professional interests, there's another awful reality: she is faced with days and days on her own, handling the same dishes, folding the same clothes, walking down the same supermarket aisles, taking the same items off the shelves, watching the same hour yield the same set of dynamics, with manic children falling out of school buses, exhausted husband pulling the car to a halt in the driveway with the same cauldron in his mind, wondering whether he really wants to be in this driveway tonight, while she is wondering if the place is even her place any more, and wondering, with the same mind, whether she really wants this particular man in her driveway tonight. Does she want an empty driveway for a change? Does she want the school bus to go floating by, filled with angels and destined for a distant planet?

A male talk-back radio show host, broadcasting nationally, was once described as: 'Our famed male millionaire radio star having a welcome breather from talking to "Mogadon-stuffed housewives" . . . ' Reading that, my heart lurched. Are these the ones with the domestic chaos, with nowhere to go during the day, no alternative focus to their lives, and no way out that they can see? Lumped together and slain in a few words? No doubt they are.

'I remember, one afternoon, Hilary and I were sitting in a bar around the corner from our other building, which was a three-storeyed house', said Diana, who was wearing a pair of black baggy pants and a pink tee-shirt. 'It was the sort

of place we would have been in when we were students. I was suddenly hit by the idea that around the corner from where we had originally been possessionless and unknowing 19 year olds, was now a big building that was filled with our children, filing cabinets, books, staff, typewriters, telephones, stationery, ideas, plans, expectations and commitments—and we had assembled it all. It's an extraordinary thing to have, and I think it represents all sorts of things in my life, to have this kind of a place'.

Hilary dived in: 'It's an odd sort of feeling to think we have created something that is now an institution'.

As I listened I was remembering Wendy McCarthy describing tried and true old marriages. She had said: 'You know, that stage you get to when you finish each other's lovemaking, and you finish each other's sentences, too'. Hilary and Diana have that ingredient in their relationship. They finish each other's sentences, understand each other's stream-of-consciousness, amplify each other's point of view, and extend each other's thoughts; and I was aware also of the subtle ducking and weaving, and Hilary's highly strung edge that is both seductive and cautioning. Her enthusiasm bore with it a sharpness.

'Maybe if we'd created a biscuit factory we'd feel the same way, but I don't think so', said Hilary, leaning forward in her black tights, skinny black skirt and loose khaki shirt. 'There's something about publishing and books, and the way we can incorporate our lives into McPhee Gribble that feels extraordinary'. I was seeing how Hilary's creative personality needed McPhee Gribble. In some other corporate context she may have lost herself in the power-play of egos, and lost sight of her essence. In this place of her own, and complemented by the constancy of Diana, her volatile soul finds appropriate expression and is simultaneously nourished by its environment. We each topped up our cups of coffee from the bright pot on the little table that separated the white sofas in Hilary's plain, book-lined office.

Don Watson sees Hilary as a perfectionist, in the sense of always trying to create 'the perfect moment'. 'She has a deep irritation with imperfection and slovenliness', he said. 'She is a creature of instinct, descended from the displaced border raiders, the McPhees from Skye, and in her ferocity she wants to avenge that loss of ancestral strength and dignity'.

He believes that Hilary 'knows' where she comes from with a great ancestral memory and connection to her roots. Her mother came from a genteel, Anglican, Tasmanian background, and her father was a Scottish banker, steeped in the hardiness of islanders. 'Hilary can offer moments of brilliance. She can make a whole room feel happy, and she is also capable of making the room want to clear out, and fast!' he said.

'Formidable' is the way Meredith, the McPhee Gribble book designer (who calls herself a 'fashion fascist') describes Hilary. Meredith regularly threatens to resign when the volatility hits the fan, and creative minds lock over issues that matter passionately to every member of staff.

While Hilary, with her 'border raiders' ancestry, feels a

need to strive to prove her worth, and to exercise the power of control if she feels she's in a corner, Diana approaches life and its gifts with more of a sense of entitlement, a sense of trust in the order of things.

Diana Glen was raised with a matter-of-fact view of life. Her early knowledge of the world was once removed. She was a Gippsland selector's daughter, at ease in the ruling class of Melbourne. Diana had been a bookworm as a little girl. From time to time she had bouts of rheumatic fever, and was confined to bed for months at a time. Her mother used to ply her with books, borrowed from here, there and everywhere, because Diana was quite happy to devour two or three books a day.

Diana describes her mother as having a special point of connection to all her children. She was a painter, and had been a student of George Bell, that great figure in the Melbourne art world of the 30s. 'But because of her background and that era, my mother's painting was never taken seriously. She always had a sense of there being another world that she might have inhabited', Diana explained. (Disciplined as she is, Diana's sense of 'entitlement' allows her to move around the office like a woman who doesn't have to work.)

On the notice-board behind Diana's desk was a photograph of a beautiful woman, and above it, one of a man and a fair-haired little girl: 'Yes, my parents', Diana said softly, following my look. 'There is a very strong link from my grandmother to my mother to me, though they were both frustrated women, tied up as they were with child-rearing, and relinquishing their talent and their desire for the other world. I think my background gave me great confidence, because I don't really care what people think of me personally. Whether they think I'm peculiar or acceptable is incidental. But I care very much what they think of my work', Diana added quietly.

Diana was raised with intense Protestant probity: a correctness with no intolerance, or greed, or ostentation, or sense of newness, just a fine sense of frugality. 'I always take notice of what Diana says to look at, whether we're in a gallery, a house, or out in the country. She has an impeccable eye, and will always spot the perfect thing to notice wherever we are'. This was said by John Timlin, who described to me how he saw her as a woman with a powerful intellect, and explained his love for her being even stronger because she didn't hide that intelligence in the manner of 'some women who believe that intelligence is not a highly sought-after sexual attribute'.

'Ours is a tempestuous relationship, that hobbles and runs and never feels artificial', he said.

Diana and Hilary taught everyone who worked for them. They've raised up school leavers and high-school drop-outs. One of the former is Meredith, their designer, now in her early thirties. She came through the doors of McPhee Gribble as a tentative researcher at the age of 17, and apprenticed herself to these two women. She has one of the keenest eyes and soundest noses in the trade. The soft beauty and poetic movement of their book designs is largely the result of Meredith's enduring work.

'This organisation requires an enormous level of performance from people', Diana said. 'People get terribly upset if they make mistakes. It's not just a "job". They are responsible for all aspects of what they do, and their pride is tied up with that, knowing they will let everyone down if they do something wrong, and knowing that every extra penny we have to spend is difficult'.

They were fairly demanding of their staff, but felt upset to see them staggering into the office after working late the previous night: 'We then have to reprimand them for working too hard, thus disguising a real need for extra help', Diana said. 'We now expect them to tell us—that's what we mean by shared management. We don't always want to be the ones to make the decision to employ freelance people or put on extras'.

They instituted a system of three managers which was like a big system grafted on to a smaller organisation. Sue Hines, who later moved to Heinemann, was the third of these managers. When I spoke to her she was McPhee Gribble's

Managing Editor. 'We all carry McPhee Gribble with us all the time', she said. 'I used to be a teacher, and could walk away from school at the end of each day. In here, it gets into the bones'.

Sue started as a trainee editor at a time when McPhee Gribble was producing twelve books a year, not fifty. 'So I am Hilary's creature, and my editing skills have come straight from her. I have been made by McPhee Gribble, and sometimes it's terrifying: but it's impossible to feel nothing about this place'. Her gratitude to Hilary was obvious.

Soft around the edges like a siren's song? I asked Diana what John Timlin might have meant by that.

'I think that being the sort of place we are, we expect people to submit to the McPhee Gribble kind of style, any time they have dealings with us'. This was matter-of-factly said. 'There is some seduction in that', she added.

One of the roles of the publisher is to be as it were the examiner. It's a powerful role, scrutinising a writer's work, and passing or failing it. 'That's a very brave thing for any writer to do', said Di. 'The publisher has the ultimate power. It's not just that of critic: it's the actual yes or no to making it available to the public at all'.

Maybe what happens to people like Hilary and Diana, as they accumulate years of practice at their art of examining, and integrate the power of examiner to such an extent that it becomes part and parcel of their personalities, is that they begin to see the world through the 'examiner's' set of lenses. I put this to Diana one afternoon. She laughed her easy, infectious laugh.

'You mean we might see the world as though it were up for acceptance or rejection? I think there's something in that! It makes me remember when I went to the fortieth birthday party of an old university friend, and one of the guests was a man I had only seen intermittently over the years. He was an actor and director. He came over to me, drunk, and he said: "One thing that never occurred to us [him and his male contemporaries] was that you two would one day judge us".'

In the early days of McPhee Gribble, the work roles of

Hilary and Diana were more or less interchangeable. Later they became more specialised in their own areas; they could deputise for each other in a general sense, but in details they no longer could. It was more valuable to McPhee Gribble for Diana to be the expert in management and design, while Hilary was the undisputed expert in fiction editing, who had developed her personal networking experience overseas.

People are pleased to see her when she alights from Australia. Ah, there is a face to McPhee Gribble! 'It's an odd feeling when I am actually presenting McPhee Gribble', said Hilary. 'I feel terribly proud of it, and I laugh inside because I know that we would fit into the foyer of most publishing houses I visit. The Simon and Schuster bathrooms are the size of my office'.

Australia is in a unique position in the English-speaking publishing world, in that it's a long way from everywhere and has been seen as the dumping ground for much publishing that has happened elsewhere. In the past twenty years it has discovered it own voice, and now 50 per cent of what Australian readers read is Australian, whereas twenty years ago it was closer to 15 per cent. Australia has become more mainstream, less a branch office: we are now less likely to be tacked on as a market eighteen months after a book has been published elsewhere.

There is still a long way to go; the Australian market is still tiny compared with everyone else's. It is Hilary's job to make sure that the rest of the world doesn't forget about McPhee Gribble. Often when she walks into agents and publishers in London and New York, she is greeted with: 'Oh, we have never met an Australian publisher before!' That is because most publishing houses in this country are British owned.

'You'd go a long way to find someone as intelligent and intuitive as Hilary', was something that I heard time and time again. It is a rare and weighty combination, and the strength of Hilary's intellect and creativity makes her particularly good at fiction, as judge and analyst.

Helen Garner, whose best-selling book *Monkey Grip* was

only the second manuscript accepted by the fledgling McPhee Gribble for publication, is now a close friend of Hilary (whom she describes as 'the explosive one with all the bombs going off') and Diana ('a calm orderly person who can ride through crises without getting ruffled'). 'Hilary is the only person I ever show my work to before it's finished', Helen said. 'I trust her and she's a terrific editor; she has a tendency to draw more out of me rather than chop things back. She's skilled at that, and has a very light touch'.

Diana's singular role is in the physical making of the book. One senses the weightiness and depth of the 'publisher' in Diana. She is a logician, a technician, and a coach. 'My dream and plan is that soon we will have a sophisticated set of computerised forecasts that will take me only a month a year to maintain', she said. She was behind the door in her office, seemingly attached to her computer terminal, programming it with data on incomings and outgoings. When focused on this task, she tuned out the human dynamic and the visual world of the building, and honed in on the scores of little green names and numbers, printing out sheets of predictions and plans.

Diana didn't like being funnelled into this isolating job. 'It doesn't feel as though it has any outcome', she said, 'other than the ongoing operation, the stability of the place. It's interesting that I can become immersed in the numbers; but it's also deeply boring'.

There was a lull in the room as Hilary and I watched Diana.

'It's a temporary phase', said Hilary, reassuringly. She was reaffirming her commitment to having Diana free of the computer; she didn't like to think of Diana glued to the monitor screen while she, Hilary, was out winning the world. And she knew how difficult Diana was finding this period. This was Australian publishing, 90s style, and they both knew how they had catapulted themselves into it.

'But I'm not sure about the tyranny of serving a set of forecasts', said Diana, 'or whether that function has to continue, and so too the tyranny'.

'Obviously we have to employ someone to monitor this

computer if its function continues to increase', said Hilary. 'Because Di has too much to offer in terms of ideas. It's like watching Di being sucked into another dimension'.

Pre-computer, Hilary and Di always had a rough plan mapped out that fitted in with the intuitive moves they made over the years. And they have always had a well-documented sales base from which to operate. Even with the computer, both remained equally involved at the planning stage of a project.

The computer was to offer a more accurate system to test ideas against. 'Our gut response won't be abandoned, but now it will be testable', said Hilary. 'Because that's all that publishing can be—it must always be an intuitive leap in the dark, because no two books are alike. And there'll still be an overlap of roles for us.'

Diana looked at us and said wryly: 'If you watch me at this computer it will be like watching grass grow . . . '

At this point, Diana's twelve-year old daughter Anna, long-haired, robust and engaging, sailed into the office, slumped her school bag down, and settled into the swing of the afternoon's atmosphere. Anna's relationship with her mother seems to be one of sisterly/motherly interchange of love and vitality. They enjoyed the exchange of the day's doings. Diana sat in her mode of crumpled attentiveness as Anna entertained us all with her observations: 'I think it's good for Mum that she works, because she's doing what she wants to do and I know she wouldn't work if she didn't want to. She loves her work so much; she'd be totally bored if she wasn't doing it'.

At this point a woman photographer came in with an idea for a local book of pictures. Hilary and Diana considered her proposal. 'It's like a terrific leap of faith to take this on', said Diana. 'A terrific idea, but no manuscript'.

How do they know when an idea is good? I wondered, as the photographer found her way out, and Hilary was leading me up the stairs to the editing loft. 'There are two ways of being attracted to a manuscript', she said, taking a deep breath. 'One is being attracted to what's being said, and the other, I think, is having a respect for how something is said—a respect for the craft. There's a pang, a slight sense of excitement that I register when I come across those manuscripts. Here are words being used in a new way. And yet I may still think that the writer writes particularly well, even if I don't like the genre he's writing in. It's worth getting a reader, because maybe it's what we're looking for and is the best of its kind. We're not saying we'll never publish 'mass market' fiction, because otherwise we could end up disappearing up our own bums, which is the danger when you own your own publishing company'.

Hilary was settling herself down on the floor beside the trainee editor Sophie, who was learning the ropes. 'And we try to make sure that the ultimate horror story, of the publishers missing, or not recognising, the ultimate manuscript, doesn't occur'. As she laughed her deep laugh, I felt she was leaving me with the laugh as her mind raced on to concentrate on the next thought; her razor-sharp mind moves quickly and disengages subliminally fast when a person or idea no longer engages her.

Hilary was listening to her junior editor's rationale for her decisions and assessment of a manuscript. They had their shoes off and Hilary moved on to her knees on the grey carpet, riffling through the manuscript. 'A lot of writers try to use us as a manuscript assessing agency', she said, 'and I can certainly appreciate their need for feedback. The McPhee Gribble editing process is subjective, but I've learned to trust my responses. Some years we process a thousand manuscripts. We have also got to try not to be too rigid a filter, so that voices with which we may not necessarily resonate can still be included in our list'.

Hilary explained that McPhee Gribble sank a lot of their resources into editorial, which is unusual in publishing. They believed that middle-brow and popular books should be well-edited, and that the strength of the McPhee Gribble backlist lay in careful editing. This editing practice developed from the beginning of the company, when it took on new writers who had not published before. In retrospect, they realise it would have been suicide to let those manuscripts go unattended.

Hilary acknowledges that it's frightening for a writer to have his words slashed, and difficult for that writer to know whether he is right or not in defending himself. There is the editor, the considered professional, and the writer always questions whether he has any objectivity left, or whether his subjective attachment impels him to fight for that phrase, or that word, or that sentence construction. It is a writer's hope that he can trust his editor, after having navigated the tricky waters of creating the piece and pulling the best material from his mind.

'We try hard to make our writers happy', said Hilary. 'This business relies on word of mouth, and often a writer will say nothing until after his book is published and there he is, saying: "I love my book, but I hate the cover", or we hear two years later that one of our writers took to the bottle because he hated something about the cover. We want to attract and keep writers. They are our best field editors'.

When times have been hard at McPhee Gribble, the nurturing personalities and intelligence of Hilary and Diana have been used as substitutes for hard cash. In those times they stayed afloat although $500,000 in capital was urgently needed.

A perennial question in publishing concerns the image a publisher presents to its customers. Hilary and Diana felt that there was a danger for McPhee Gribble to be seen as occupying exclusively the 'up-market' end of Australian literature. They did also publish books which made enough money to enable the organisation to stand on the high moral ground without going bankrupt. Among their recent bestsellers have been *Dr Turf's Guide to Better Punting*, Kaz Cooke's two *Modern Girl's Guide*, and *The Practical Australian Gardener*.

'We only publish the books that we can bear to publish', emphasised Hilary. 'Someone at McPhee Gribble has to absolutely love the book, or the book idea, before we will consider taking it on'.

A delivery boy came through the double doors, out of the

rain, struggling under the weight of several cases of grog. The phone had eased off in the past half-hour. Evening was drawing in at McPhee Gribble, and Diana buffed up some glasses and put them on a tray. The company was throwing a little party for Rod Jones, who tonight was a celebrity. His novel, *Julia Paradise*, had gone into its fourth translation, and the Oslo edition had just arrived. Diana and Hilary sat side by side on a sofa. Diana poured herself a whisky with a shot of water. Hilary leaned forward and dipped into the chip bowl.

Talking to Rod about how to get around being taxed on writing-prize money, they moved into yet another dimension of the McPhee Gribble art-form. 'Have you got a good window to work next to?' Diana asked the novelist. 'So you can go in there and try to subdue your fear of writing?'

Rod's wife stood behind him, with one arm locked up between their round little baby's legs in an effort to pacify the child enough so that his father could concentrate on the meeting. The women brought a sense of festivity to this family occasion, and good wishes abounded. Soon Rod Jones and his wife and baby made ready to leave. McPhee Gribble was their lifeline, the source of their income.

Hilary and Diana were weary. The staff gathered around, talking and enthusing, their energy a bit like that at a family table when the kids tell tales of school. The two women are energised by the younger staff members. Mindful of their attention, they are silently training their staff to work through the day's doings, and thus to solidify the pattern of being self-directed.

Then it was the younger ones' turn to sit back and absorb. The two elders became vivacious again, making clear points interspersed with relaxed joking. They were well practised in creating this spontaneous forum. One by one the staff peeled off, into the night.

'Ours feels like a very experienced friendship', said Diana. 'And it knows when to leave itself alone. Even if we had a terrible fight and separated, I think, for me at least I would understand why it had happened, and it wouldn't diminish my respect or feeling for Hilary at all. We may never speak to each other again, but I know that my opinion of Hilary would never change now, regardless'. Diana and Hilary rested their eyes on each other.

'I can't imagine an incident that would leave me revising my opinion of Diana', Hilary said. 'That opinion is absolute, and will remain forever. Nor can I imagine never seeing her again. We're pretty good at making up!'

Were their rows professional?

'No; it can be all sorts of things. Sometimes I blow up for no apparent reason, other than stress and tiredness, my own tension', said Diana, who always has the suggestion of a wry little smile on her face, even if it isn't actually there.

'Diana is much better than I am at not bristling. She's better at hiding her prickliness', said Hilary.

It would be too simplistic to characterise the partnership between Hilary and Diana as a male-female duality, though if it were drawn that way, certainly Hilary would be the more aggressive, dominant and controlling partner, and Diana the more gentle, humorous and incisive. There is a strong potency to Hilary's professionalism, emanating excitement and sexuality. In her dealings with the world she tends to use her power in a controlling way; yet when she approaches a manuscript, the empathy that she forms with the writer comes through the soul of her being, and her controlling impulse is tempered by love. In that alignment of soul and ego, she is at her most potent.

Hilary said: 'Sometimes I get a terrible pang—I may be driving along in the car—and I'll think: "My God! maybe next week Diana will say that she doesn't want to do this any more". Or maybe I'll say it because I'm exhausted. And it's a pang of terror at the prospect of not being "the pair" any more. Yet we both know that each of us could manage alone if we had to. I wouldn't have said that five years ago, but I know if Di or I dropped dead the company would not stop'.

Diana moved back into the conversation. 'I think that part of the reason we have survived, particularly over this professionalisation stage, is that we have known when not to take things and gnaw them over. We can't neglect our friendship, but it doesn't have to be nursed all the time'.

It is difficult for women in their late forties who spent years as young women being exposed to the revival of feminism, and who became fully involved in professions, to pull off successful marriages. It is a terrific strain, and in many such cases it is not possible to have a domestic relationship with a man. Ideas absorbed from their professions and from feminism during that span of 15 to 18 years make domestic partnership hard for professional women. The fertility and persistence of those ideas generate more ideas, and act as a subtle and often tragic stumbling block to marital calm.

As the women talked, my eyes landed on a pile of books on the desk behind Hilary. They seemed to reflect the women. They were beautiful, compact, intricate and interesting: Helen Garner's *Postcards from Surfers*; Morris Lurie's *The Night We Ate the Sparrow*; Barney Roberts's *Tales I Carry With Me* and *Where's Morning Gone*; Bruce Pascoe's *Fox*; Kaz Cooke's *Modern Girl's Guide to Safe Sex*; and Suzanne Spunner's *Running Up A Dress*—a recognisable and distinguished stack.

'What is it that drives me to keep going?' asked Hilary of us both. 'I keep asking myself that with no true answer. The demands and effort that go into it are huge. I know the reason is that McPhee Gribble is unstoppable. It's too difficult to say that I haven't got the energy or the grit to keep going. Deciding not to go on would have to come out of external circumstances, like selling up, or some personal catastrophe. I would see it as a failure of nerve if we gave up—and in a way, that's a terrible burden to carry'.

If these two women had been in top jobs in big publishing houses, and had achieved there their arguably the best book list in Australia, they would probably not see giving that up as failure, or failure of nerve. They would put it down to circumstance.

Diana interjected: 'It's also a failure of nerve to have the feeling that this place is unstoppable. That's a failure of nerve. It gets you both ways. It would feel like a failure of nerve not to go on, and it also seems like a huge failure of nerve if we both felt at some point that this place was too draining and had stopped being a creative, productive endeavour; to not have the personal and individual courage to separate from the organisation and say "enough". Now that would be filled with nerve. It would be a brave and intelligent thing for us both to say "enough".'

'Even currently?' I asked.

'Well yes, maybe. This is something we have been doing for a huge part of our working lives, and there is some exhaustion', said Diana, quietly. Then she added: 'This is interesting! We haven't talked about this before'.

'We have sideways conversations with each other from time to time', said Di, 'during which we give each other permission to stop. That's about as far as we go. Maybe, God needs to say: "Ready, set, go!" and then we will down tools together. But maybe that's not what we want to do'.

They know that they will always be financially fragile, because they have never put the requirements of capital before the personal and organisational requirements of the place. Their priority has always been a good way to work, and to make books worth doing. So Hilary and Diana don't cherish fantasy futures, post-McPhee Gribble. 'I know that over there, there is another country called Not Going to Work At McPhee Gribble, but I am also realising that what I am doing now is me. I am where I thought I might be when I grew up, and I become more and more comfortable with that', said Diana, adding that she still feels as she did when she was 23. 'I always get a big shock when I catch sight of myself in a window or in the mirror and I think "My God! is that how I look? I only feel 23!" And I look at other women on the street and think "Oh, you're about 46"—and remind myself that that is probably how other people see me. And I will grow into an active, reliable older woman, sitting under a bauhinia tree, writing a book and having a snooze'.

Hilary, too, is comfortable when confronting the ageing process, and feels her heightened intuitive sense flow on into some kind of ability to respond to the world on a spiritual level. 'I can't put a straitjacket around that', Hilary said, 'but it is a spiritual dimension to my life that I welcome'.

Don Watson says: 'I don't think you can understand Hilary without understanding that religious dimension to her. Hilary has a natural inclination to add a touch of some ancient magic to any given situation. It could be an average Wednesday in Melbourne, and somewhere in Hilary's mind would hover a sense that the day contained the glory of a series of Epiphanies. It's natural for her spirit to be at that level, and she gets frustrated if she has to lower that standard.'

Softly, tongue in cheek, Hilary said: 'Well, Diana and I do sometimes describe ourselves as heroines to each other. It's like being strapped to the prow of a ship, knowing that we'll come out at the end of the journey as a very soaked figurehead—with the colours all running'.

POSTSCRIPT

Less than twelve months after McPhee Gribble established themselves as a fully independent publisher, Hilary and Diana's fear that their business was 'unstoppable' proved unfounded. It was announced that McPhee Gribble Publishing had been sold to Penguin Books, their long-time distributor.

Under the terms of the sale, Hilary was to be employed as a consultant by Penguin, while the McPhee Gribble list would continue to appear as an imprint of the Penguin organisation.

The difference between this new arrangement and the earlier co-publication deal with Penguin was that there was no longer room for two principals in the running of the imprint. Of the two, Diana chose to leave. Another term of the sale was that Diana sold her surname as a part of the imprint: she will not be able to use the name 'Gribble' professionally for the next two years.

The two women's telephone voices had a faraway, hollow ring when I spoke to them again in the period after the contract signing. It was as though each was saying: 'Are we still relevant?'

Hilary and Diana had faced a decision, and a process, we all go through in varying disguises—the nerve to keep going versus the nerve to give up. They had established a place that would be termed 'kindness in publishing' in many a valedictory speech, but the returns from that kindness had reached a point where they both knew they would have to consider their future.

They looked at their projections over lunch ('You usually do these things over lunch', said Diana) at the Clare Castle Hotel, and saw that although 'we had probably one of our best ever lists coming up in a year, we still couldn't sustain the kind of operation we wanted to have'. At that moment, Diana continued, 'We both converged absolutely and made an absolutely unanimous decision'.

After fifteen years of creative friendship, the two women are to be separated. 'I think it is terribly painful', Hilary said, 'like any change; but it's nothing like a marital breakdown or a death. I know I can do without Di just as I know she can survive without me. We know we'll miss the richness of the way we have worked together. I'm very sad that it has had to change, but obviously it has to change. Things can't go on forever. The fact that the jointness is now going to go out it I find very painful.'

The deal with Penguin was conditional upon Hilary being attached to the list. 'I was seen as adding value to the purchase price and I found this absolutely the hardest thing I have ever had to do in my whole life', she says now. With regard to Diana: 'I feel as though I have stolen someone's life's work, in a way. I also feel as if I have been sold, so I am absolutely split over the two things.'

She recognises that it was her creative friendship with Diana which kept the business hanging on as long as it did: 'If there had been just one of us I think we would have given up the ghost years ago. It has been changing and evolving over the last 15 years, and would have continued to change and evolve over the next five years if we had managed to go on. We both knew we had the option of cutting back to the size it was ten years ago and surviving—but that would have meant undoing all the work and all the achievement. So we chose not to turn back into what we were, but to recognise what we have become and to try and find ways of being creative in another environment'.

By now Hilary and I were talking in my agent's office in Sydney. She had come up from Melbourne to attend a 'Farewell to McPhee Gribble' party, where her achievements had been feted, and despite the air of celebration she seemed vulnerable.

'Over the last month,' she says, 'the whole business has gone through so many extraordinary cycles, where I have gone from thinking I'll have my head cut off for thinking I can still actually make something creative of this.' Her courage in the face of these conflicts is outstanding, though at one stage she says: 'Having gone through a very difficult time I would like to just fly away.'

Hilary has undergone dramatic changes in her life in the past year, with her home life paralleling the new situation for McPhee Gribble: like her business, her marriage to Don Watson has continued, but is 'simply housed in a different way'.

'I've done a huge amount of thinking and working on all this stuff', Hilary says. 'I feel terribly envious of Diana because by this dreadful body blow that has happened I haven't got the option to actually go out and do things I want to do now. I have to postpone that for another two years. Diana and I felt terribly uncomfortable for the first 24 hours. We suddenly had a burst of sniping at each other over something quite minor, and fortunately we had the wit to see there was something major behind it. We just sat in the office and had a couple of scotches and bawled like babies.'

The contract with Penguin means that Hilary's other ambitions—these include writing, and simply exploring herself as a person—will have to be put aside for at least two years. It may be longer: 'I don't know how seductive making something work again is going to be'.

Power is an element in that seduction, and yet Hilary says: 'I don't feel powerful. I am well aware that people perceive me as a person with a lot of power, but I do not want the kind of power that gives you ultimate control. I don't think it is an ultimately creative way to work. I don't think it brings out the best in people or demands the best of yourself. It is actually a rather dark side of human nature, the powerful side. The side I am interested in is . . . ' She interrupted herself. 'Words are so pathetic'.

Searching among her stock of words, some of them not as 'pathetic' as she thought, Hilary talked about the importance of a sense of history, and about the patterns which repeat themselves in the human psyche. The kind of power she had enjoyed, she felt, was one which merely provided the soil for creativity to flourish in. She was postponing the use of the word which had stopped the flow of her talk.

When I asked her if she meant to refer to the integration of the soul and the ego, she replied: 'Absolutely. I think of soul as the creative spark in the human being. It certainly is in me. It is like a little light in there that can actually start to beam or it can flicker and die. I don't know why I am so upset about it. Of course I don't fear it is going to flicker and die, but I really don't want to postpone its development. Without that little light we are really just husks . . . '

Hilary rearranged herself in her director's chair. She brushed the tears from her cheek. She got up and moved softly around the carpeted space. She didn't shy away from the poignant moment she had fallen into.

She was telling of a choice, which events had made for, between the pursuit of the personal and the nurturing of the creative spark in others through the medium of large corporate publishing . . .

The day before I spoke to Hilary, Diana, who was also in Sydney for the farewell party, spent the morning with me. Languid in soft silk clothes, she was relaxed and forthcoming. She ran her fingers through her hair—a nonchalant habit of hers—and talked about the excitement she felt for the future, and about her feelings of loss.

'I feel as though Hilary is carrying the burden', she said. 'But she feels guilty too. She told me that she feels as though she is stealing my life's work. What we decided was that we had to wrap up what we had learnt from each other like two parcels, with beautiful paper and ribbons and bows and birds and balloons, and give them to each other. So we did this, saying: "Here it is, take it—it is yours to do whatever you like with".'

This gestalt ritual helped both of them to get through the anger and anguish of separation. 'When you work so closely with someone', said Diana, 'and get torn apart, you find out which is you and which is her. I was stunned and frightened, and thought What can I do? There is nothing I can do. I can't do anything; I'm only half of a person. Or I didn't even know if I was half. I thought maybe I was anywhere from nothing to 30 per cent of the mix.'

These feelings of panic passed quickly as Diana found that she was intensely interested in the process of discovering herself. 'In the process', she says, 'Hilary and I have had some terrific talks, probably the best talks we've had for years. There is some tension that has gone out of the relationship.'

I remembered something Hilary had told me a year before, of feeling a terrible pang as she drove to work, thinking: 'My God, what if Diana doesn't want to do it any more?' Diana had responded to this: 'I used to feel sick driving to work just with the sheer tension of keeping it all together.'

In the last two years of their partnership, Diana found herself forced to take the accountant's side, at a time when it felt as if the place was being subverted by accountants. 'I know the finances in more detail', she said, 'so they were more at the front of my head. I was always having to hold up a magnifying glass to it, or run a ruler over it, which was awful for Hilary. It was awful for me. It was awful for everybody.'

The discovery Diana has been making, she said, 'is what I really am capable of as an individual. I don't think I will ever again feel quite so entangled, or quite so unsure of which bits are me and which bits aren't. I think this separation experience is quite a crucial one.'

In the separation, and in the time she has taken to consider her next move, Diana has begun to question where true fulfilment lies for her. It should have something to do, she thinks, with 'the coming together of an action with an intention. The intention is something to do with self.'

In the future she means to keep her intentions—meaning her soul, or self—intact. In the meantime, while she is, as she says, 'a non-person at the moment', 'it feels pleasant and freeing. I am astonished at how much I can actually read. I can do things that I haven't been able to do for so long because of the pressure. It feels terrific, though every now and again I feel guilty, as if I am betraying things. Perhaps my feelings of happiness and freedom are just a way of not thinking about the sadness—about the place not being there any more. But it feels as though anything can happen. It's like getting younger. I have that enormous kind of optimism you have in your 20s.'

Diana's intentions have always been, she says, 'about making ideals sustainable'. She has the conviction 'that somehow you can do things that are worth doing—you can communicate ideas that really have something to offer to more people than just a tiny group. That is what success is. It is not about earning money. It is about . . . '

Like Hilary, Diana seemed hesitant when she came to the point of describing the essence of her being: 'I think we just don't have the language for it. We don't have a vocabulary for it. The expression that people feel comfortable with is the idea of grace. I find it very interesting, being in a state of grace or not. Perhaps you go on from there and do a full circle and come back to being able to use the words "soul" and "spiritual".'

Diana is reluctant to talk about her future plans in any detail, except to say: 'I imagine myself doing something quite quietly'. Yet her daughter Anna, who knew how much Diana loved her work, is nervous about this: Diana thinks 'she has this nightmare vision of me crouching in the house, waiting for her to get home in order to ply her with questions'.

That vision is not going to happen. Though she does not expect to replicate her work situation at McPhee Gribble— 'I don't want to get myself into a situation where I am diverted by other people's imagination'—she remains 'terribly interested in groups and organisations—in how they work and how things can be structured so that there can be direction but freedom.'

Now, she says, 'I would like to think there was more space in my life for having a two-way exchange of feeling with people. I have always been looking at my watch and thinking, Have I got time to talk to this person? I would like to think I can stop feeling engulfed by other people. My hope is that I can avoid being cynical. In the past I have been suspicious of people who have said they loved me: I felt, What does this person want from me? I would like to be more relaxed about it, and not assume all the time that to have a relationship with someone means to be completely submerged.'

Diana was relaxed as she reflected on the personal empowerment which comes from a balanced self-love. She no longer fears being taken over by people, as she now feels the power to say: 'You cannot have that from me', or 'That belongs to me'.

'Over the next couple of months', Diana said, 'I would like to work out how to use all the experience I have got. My feeling is that if I can't do something really high-minded that feels wonderful, I'd rather do something completely different, like work in a bank. Perhaps when this book comes out I'll be working in a sandwich bar—making every sandwich a good one.'

Jane Singleton

'WELCOME BACK, YOU'RE FIRED'

Jane Singleton, the woman, is softly spoken. Her speech is quick, and clear-minded. She uses short, strong sentences, throwing in an occasional swear-word in a natural, to-make-a-point, Aussie fashion. She is sensual and attractive. Her body is tall and relaxed, with curvy hips that are comfortable and girlish in a full cotton skirt, matronly and efficient in a black pleated one. She has sexy legs whether she's barefooted or in her trademark black stockings and high heels. She has acutely attentive eyes, capable hands, undressed-up nails, and kissable lips, especially when her two little children are around her. And she puts her shoulder pads on her desk when she's finished being public!

Jane Singleton, the journalist, is a toey, edgy personality. She's an issue-based journalist, clever and highly strung. She's not a glad hand. She's defensive and somewhat threatened by workmates. She is sometimes difficult. Her insecurity is a thread that runs through the fabric of her nature. Her mind works in top gear. She is prickly when other minds are what she calls 'dozy', and when real information is not forthcoming.

Jane has the rare and powerful combination of a strong, sensitive, penetrating, energetic intellect, blended with guts and heart. She is funny, with an easy laugh when she is relaxed. Her interest and determination with issues, which many Australians may not identify with, springs from extensive travels and a probing curiosity for the politics of other places. Jane is compassionate. She has had friends disappear overnight, never to resurface from jails or death. Her husband David was initiated into the ways of Jane's rebellious drive when he had to smuggle her out of Brazil in the boot of his car. She had put herself on the line with her journalism.

Jane has been married to David Singleton for fifteen years. David is fair-haired, gentle and precise. He is a warm-hearted man who guards his family. He knows that Jane is a shy woman; he's the one who gives her a pill and a drink before a party, propels her there and pats her down. David is at ease with his own value and finds media hype, interference and cruelty hard to take. Jane tries to protect David from her external media life, and David does his best to protect Jane from herself—and from the strain of being that shy person, who in her public life has fallen prey to an excessive amount of media scrutiny and slamming.

Why? Possibly because Jane is confrontative, both as a woman of intellectual rigour and as one of the most professional journalists in Australia. She is dedicated to the principle of journalistic insightfulness; she's not one to bury the lead. She's prepared to forfeit little for that commitment. Her following comprises a large, often silent, questioning and thoughtful segment of Australia's population.

In 1988 Jane Singleton, the journalist, hit the footpath for the second time in six months. The first time had been her sacking from her job as anchor for the ABC's *7.30 Report* in Sydney; ABC sources told the press at the time that Jane needed to be 'feminised and humanised'.

Subsequently, Jane was offered John Laws's morning program at the Sydney commercial radio station 2GB. It was to be the first female attempt at the morning time-slot vacated by the rich prince of the airwaves.

Five months into her show, Jane and David and the kids were holidaying on the remote central Queensland property of old friends. Disrupting the atmosphere of a place with no power and no water, 2GB tracked Jane down at the homestead by phone. The message was that she was fired, and would she please come and empty out her office on her return to Sydney.

This edict pounded through the mind of the radio station's new 'darling', who had been employed because of her distinction as a personality who could think. Big money had been spent on advertising her introduction as one of the first women to do mornings on a commercial station.

The pressure was on. Jane, who had spent twelve years with the ABC, was facing the thunder all commercial media personalities face: the dilemma of having just two audience surveys in which to prove themselves. Beyond that, their career futures become anybody's guess.

By her second survey, the 2GB station ratings had plummeted, and Jane's program was targeted for blame, with no disclosure made as to the real reason for this. Her audience was left in the lurch as it had been when she left the ABC, feeling short-changed at yet another disappearance.

Her treatment has been curious. There she was, running a current affairs program for the ABC, the one media outlet that supposedly rewards professionalism and quality journalism, and she was told her that it had been decided to cull the

WOMEN OF POWER

women and replace her with a man. All those being considered for her job were interviewed within sight of Jane as she worked. The process took long, drawn-out, blood-letting months. In the words of a devoted minder from those television days, Jane was fired 'with a wedge in her chest', and replaced by a woman (not a man).

Jane may well have had cause to wonder whether the decision was taken exclusively by management, or whether her fellow journalists were consulted and concurred with their bosses. Concurrence with the bosses is unfortunately a common practice in contemporary Australian journalism, especially for those who want to have a future. Jane herself hosted an Australian Journalists Association International Conference in early 1989, at which one of the discussions focused on censorship, and the level of self-censorship practised by journalists worldwide (and in particular those employed by Rupert Murdoch's News Limited) in order to feel assured of their jobs.

This calls into question the collective self-esteem of journalists, and their tendency not to recognise and reward professionalism within their own ranks. Do they really have such little regard for themselves? The shadow side of the ebullient, life-and-soul-of-the-party, knowledgeable and confident journo is all too frequently a personality wracked by self-doubt, constantly aspiring to impossible levels of excellence, while feeling in the quietness of the soul a persistent sense of fraudulence and inadequacy.

They tend to value each other for being self-effacing rather than for having a healthy chunk of self-worth. They rank poorly in research surveys, like used-car salesman and politicians. They tend to allow the predominantly negative public view of their occupation to colour their views of themselves and sometimes of each other; they are constantly being questioned on the level of their integrity and this would get to anyone during a public career. And it's as though they have succumbed to that negative image, rather than impressing the public with their worth as individuals and creators of quality product.

The researching and shadowing of Jane was done in the days when she was just beginning to feel settled at 2GB. She had worked with a couple of producers, and was now attempting to strengthen the rhythm and pace within her all-female team.

Their day began at 6 a.m. The women converged on their suite of offices that overlooked the city. They pored over the papers, plucked stories, checked the satellite news, and sifted through thoughts amongst themselves as the radio plunked away with its morning urgency. The women, with creased morning faces, honed in on ideas, took some points to extremes, sent each other up, laughed, delegated phone calls and began to shape the three-hour Jane Singleton Show.

Traffic picked up slowly below. Jane sat with her legs folded under her, springing forth with ideas and automatically tempering them, mentally pacifying the station. Photos of her children waved about on their drawing pins, blowing in the draught of the central heating system.

'He's such a pain in the arse', she said, putting down the phone receiver on some human being who was rudely reluctant to illuminate the story of the Redfern Aboriginal people's scuffle the night before. Jane had decided to give the story high profile.

She sorted through material from her researchers, linking things together and pulling the best pieces from a stream of details, while imparting a solidity, enthusiasm and information to her team, who were awaiting direction. All the while she was preparing to go on air in as stress-free a state as possible.

It seemed that Jane had intelligence, wit and drive coursing through her system, with no-one there as an equal to hitch up to; no one to prune and propel her progress; to help harness and respect that energy, and nurture it for optimum performance. And there was a mood within the team, which Jane had to cope with, of 'just having a joke'. Sometimes this seemed to frustrate and distract her, since this was not a comedy show; on the other hand, she is good at melting

JANE SINGLETON

her face and swooping into a belly-laugh at some dirty talk or clever insight that her producer would throw at her for good measure.

Jane has the energy of a high-spirited, clever, young mare, with a wildness and vulnerability such that if she had to run the course for too long alone, without feedback and comfort, she may well be done in. During the period of a week she went from having a mild sniffle to a fully fledged 'flu, which no doubt had something to do with her sense of isolation.

Jane had been somewhat rocked by a slice of cruelty in the press that morning, likening her persistence with politicians to that of a terrier. Guided by her resourceful wit, she had asked her soundman to find some taped barking of little dogs, and requested that it be fed through the introduction to her program.

Dialogue with her team about the program they were about to put to air continued, with Jane building on the determination in the room, until each person had enthusiasm to go to the phones and extract agreements from high-profile 'talent'—people in that morning's news—to be a part of that day's *Jane Singleton Show*.

'Yes, darling, it's me'. Jane had answered her insistent phone. 'I gave Tommy and Jess their worm medicine last night. It's in the little yellow bottle and they can take it now. You all right? O.k. darling. Yes, I'm o.k. No, I've got my nose stuff. O.k., darling. Bye'.

It was David, doing a little more guarding. Jane designs it so that her domestic life overlaps her professional life. She is comfortable with it that way. It gives her confidence and the warmth she needs, to ease the isolation. The phone rang again.

'What's wrong, darling baby? He isn't your friend any more? Did you chase him? Maybe you were too rough for him. Do you want to go to school today? Are you sure? All right, baby. Is Daddy there? Can I speak to him? Goodbye, baby'.

She checked her watch and swivelled around to her typewriter to compose the morning's editorial on the Aboriginal story. The huge mural of laughing kookaburras on a correspondingly tall city building opposite the window became suffused with glare, then faded as the sun climbed closer to nine o'clock.

'Is there anyone important enough for me to put on make-up for?' Jane asked the team of women who were completing the morning's time-sheet. She folded her hands gently across her middle as she asked. She was becoming more gentle as her on-air time approached, wanting some nurturing support, some soothing in readiness.

She stood behind the door where there was a tiny mirror, and slowly made up her face. 'Sad not being made-up any more', she said quietly, remembering her television days.

Suddenly there was an organised shuffling of papers and the team collected its material, waited for Jane and filed up the stairs to take their positions in the studio and control booth for the next three hours.

Jane rolled into the show, smooth and nimble. She was toey, and it added a thread of excitement. She was challenging the listener to think along with her. She was confronting an area manager for Telecom, who had been recruited to do the interview by his superiors, but had no brief on the subject of Jane's gripe. In no time she had him admitting that he didn't know why he was there, and had no pertinent answers to her questions. She was voicing the chagrin of the public. She made constant eye contact with her producer through the glass, needing the connection. To the Telecom man, she was hospitable yet reproachful; calm, yet challenging.

Ushering him out, Jane rose. Leaning over the controls, she shook hands with her next guest, a politician. They sized each other up while a taped commercial went to air, giving Jane a rare off-the-air breathing space in her three-hour marathon. She introduced her interviewee, tolerated his smoothly prepared presentation for just long enough, and then got on with the nitty-gritty of her questioning.

Jane's supporters claim to feel represented by her voice, which shoots straight, with an educated style and the sort of precision that one desires from a friend who is trying to get to the heart of a matter. It affords them relief that somebody's out there doing it on their behalf.

'This is entertainment; it's the city looking up its own arse. He's certainly got "get into bed and get onya" eyes', the producer said in her gravelly voice, grinning at her own style of making cracks. Her macho-fashion send-up lightened the atmosphere where yet another Australian politician was displaying the archetypal political waffle.

When a journalist such as Jane takes on one of these, the public tendency is to take the politician's side. Maybe this is part of middle Australia's primary school conditioning that the teacher is exempt from error or blame. Yet who is the teacher—the politician or the journalist? It augurs badly for journalism if we automatically see the pollies as the authorities.

On the other side of the glass, Jane drank water. Her cheeks were flushed. She stood and welcomed her next guest, a small man with a knighthood, who dealt in 'procedures'.

'This is going to be like shovelling shit uphill with a slotted spoon', said the producer. 'The likes of Laws are not about stimulating the mind and getting an audience to think for itself. They're about telling the audience what to think'. She knew that Jane would do her darnedest to startle this titled gentleman into some sort of debate and keep the collective audience mind popping, rather than offering it a brain message.

Jane has the capacity to encourage the listener to pay closer attention. But since the average listener's attention span is reportedly between three and eight minutes, her method of journalism is a challenge. If only a middle Australian listener could stay with Jane's method, he might be wooed into experiencing provocation of thought: that would be a nifty achievement in this age of man as the spectator.

Is Jane too serious? What person has everything in their armoury? Yet she is a serious person, contributing more than many of her colleagues, her mind and conscience always at work.

Next, Jane was exposing yet another flustered and unprepared man, an alderman. The engineer played with the controls and set a background sound with Jane's new audio-logo, the sound of the yapping terrier mixed with a baby crying.

'I'll rip what's left of his ageing nuts off', said the producer to a research assistant who had just appeared with a telephone complaint. She shifted her attention back to Jane. 'Is Jane sick? She's white-knuckling it a bit, isn't she?' The producer was no longer kidding.

Jane's voice came through the speakers: 'I'm not prepared to say what I guarantee to ask a politician', she said firmly, maintaining a very levelled eye on her alderman. 'I don't think we can address a minister and not the issues that concern him'.

The seriousness of her delivery is softened by a sense that

JANE SINGLETON

Jane is coming from a place of unremitting personal integrity. Whether she is ill, angered, lonely, or defensive, there is reassurance in her willingness to reveal herself and stay on the mark.

'I have specific views on journalism', said Jane later, as she ate a sumptuous lunch in the open courtyard of a city restaurant. She had done eight hours straight on just a cheese sandwich and glasses of water. 'I try not to change those views, and don't believe I should. If I'm dealing with a politician, I know he is there to do a job; he has a sacred trust in terms of public information. I'm not going to have it flirted away. If I'm there to interview an entertainer, who's quite pleasant and answerable for very little in the world, then fine; but not someone who must be answerable to the media'.

Jane's greatest skill is that of an interviewer, whether for radio or television. She is one of the few people who can handle long, revealing interviews with people who have something to say and who need to be put on the spot. Jane is sensitive to the fact that she is unable to carry that hard-hitting interviewer's clarity into any combat between herself and management. She will shy away from confrontation, preferring negotiation. She finds an enormous difference between selling herself and selling a product or soliciting information.

She knows that to be effective she has to be able to sell herself. She's convinced that men are better trained to talk about their own value. Women, particularly those of Jane's age—into their forties and older—find that more difficult. She would be the first to acknowledge that in a sharp-edged interview she is asserting the value of the industry, but when it came to dealing with management for her own defence, she had qualms about her innate value, and little confidence in her approach.

Her commitment is to a quality product. Quality information is one of the most liberating elements in any country. It serves to enlighten the public consciousness and to diminish prejudice. We have a perception of quality as it relates to consumer goods, but we don't apply the same criteria to information. A good journalist applies her brain to a complicated issue, knowing that it can't be simplified because it will blow away then and nobody will understand it; nevertheless, she will explain it as best she can. Inevitably, when a journalist does her research, she moves through various levels of truth.

She might start by finding that this person appears to be a saint, but after more research she may get a perception of him as a sinner; then after further investigation, as she begins to understand the system that encourages the person to sin, she gets closer to an understanding of the psychopathology that makes up the dualistic framework of his behaviour. It means hard work and hard thinking; once the journalist herself is clear about the issue, there's still plenty of footwork involved in interpreting the ambiguities to the audience.

Many journalists realise when they start out that they will get paid the same for a quiet life as they will for tearing themselves to bits. Jane is one who has been inclined to put herself to the test, often tearing herself to pieces. Her mother had died just a couple of weeks before these interviews took place. Jane is an only child. Her mother, who was a great beauty, was separated from her husband when Jane was a baby. She started her own clothing manufacturing business in the 1940s, and was a woman whose independence has been a strong influence on Jane's life.

Throughout her mother's illness, Jane flew back and forth to her bedside, all the while presenting the *Jane Singleton Show* from unfamiliar studios in Melbourne. She nursed her mother through to her death. David held the family fort with Jess and Tommy.

These were the early days of her radio show. She was being supported only minimally by 2GB in having some of her idiosyncratic wishes granted. There is still enormous resistance to working women paying attention to their domestic and family lives, and very little help offered for a holistic approach to living which encompasses career and family and acknowledges that both men and women have to cope with both, with one or the other coming to prominence in their lives at different times. To make demands is a quick way to test the parameters of surrounding support and ascertain how far one can go.

To Jane, it seemed that she was not allowed the excesses that are afforded male stars. There she was, the one woman whose photograph hung in the big portrait gallery at reception, the radiant girl who could think—but if she made any fuss because the air conditioning didn't work in her cubicle, she would be ignored.

Was that because she was a woman? Or was it because she was new? Was it trial by fire? Was it because her determination to be a significant presence to her family while continuing her career had already caused some hackles to rise?

It's a wise, confident, and almost certainly male radio star who walks out of the studio if the talk-back lines fail to function efficiently. That star who acts out the child, makes the demands, and has them met, feels confident actively to create an aura of indispensability around himself. That way he creates a world in which there is minimal interference from management and in which most whims are acknowledged and the ego is continually assuaged. Of course, if you want your soul taken care of too, that's a tall order.

Jane said that she wasn't accustomed to the way she might have exerted her power. Her ego is more tempered than that of one male colleague, who kicked down doors if he felt it would make a point. Does female conditioning keep us in line and remind us to 'just go along with it'? Do we tend to lack the confidence to create that aura which spells out: 'Respect me or else!'?

Jane said that she had to ask two, three, or four times for the same thing, either being ignored, or being reacted to as 'demanding'.

'So', she said, 'it was clear that the strategy was to behave like a deadshit, in order to get things to happen. I still have to work out whether I am prepared to carry on with that sort of superstar act. I'd rather negotiate. People think of me as a demanding sort of person anyway', she added. 'I believe it's the perception that men choose to promulgate about women'.

Media women believe that they must be twice as good as men at what they do, and must have a stronger sense of morality than men, to survive in the male domain. There are many men, who still believe that women with children at home should not be out working.

Jane believes that 2GB had expectations of her behaviour as a woman rather than as a person. The TV ad for her radio program, showing Jane, her legs sheathed in seamed stockings and feet in stilettos, walking away from the camera, testifies to that. For Jane in that position, so much time and effort was used up on subtle and extraneous demands, ducking and weaving in order to maintain her position.

Many of the high rollers in radio are reputed to be extraordinarily frightened. They are men who have made big money, who live on the raw energy of radio, with its exposed nerves and anxiety, and who don't have the anchor of an ideology. Some of these people act like weathercocks. They sense what the public wants and point in that direction. It's the opportunism of male ranters who live in dread of the next rating.

To these people, women are often seen as threatening. Not only may they be attractive, but they may be women who feel outraged at injustice, find absurdity in protecting criminals, and are not prepared to avoid the truth.

'Woman are more honest, and more prepared to give decent answers', said investigative journalist Chris Masters, who, after fifteen years in the business, also says: 'I will always try to get to the women when I'm after some of the hardest-to-come-by truth'.

Chris, who has known Jane for all those years, respects her brand of journalism which he says exemplifies her personal integrity. He knows that to Jane words and ideas are important, and that that may slow her down and make her less entertaining, more lacking in frivolity. There are those who would say that these are the reasons that Jane was ousted; not because she is a beautiful, brainy woman who takes her role and the issues seriously. But there were other on-air people at 2GB who had worse ratings and who are still there.

Radio is a consummately ephemeral and unstable business. The cyclic testing of ratings comes round every three months, and their effect is to make or break people's lives. The consequence is that there are constant and tremendous upheavals throughout all levels in radio, not least at the highest level of management. The ricochet, through each station, and the industry at large, is devastating.

Moves at senior executive level in metropolitan stations, according to major industry surveys, are unbelievably high. In 1988, of the nine Sydney commercial stations, three of the top executives were struck off. In Melbourne, of nine stations, five top executives bit the dust. Of the six Brisbane stations, half the management staff were dropped and replaced. In Adelaide, of the five stations, three executives disappeared, During Jane's five months of employment at 2GB, ownership of the station changed three times.

With that happening at senior executive level, it's easy to see the cause of the upheavals among radio station managers, program directors, journalists and announcers. It's tragic for the industry that under the influence of ratings surveys, many good people are destroyed and lost, especially when it could be that announcers are just the fall-guys for radio stations whose direction gets lost in management shakedowns and ownership changes. The victims may or may not be responsible for a ratings burn but the ratings hit like napalm and many are scarred as well as having to wear the shame of being dumped.

Little wonder that it's an industry filled with frightened management and frightened talent. The effect of such high attrition rates is violent and all-pervasive. One never knows:

rooster today, feather duster tomorrow!

It was shown by the second survey during Jane's time at 2GB that the ratings for the whole station had gone down.

It would normally be argued that a morning person would be dependent on the breakfast person; that it might, in fact, have been the breakfast person who pulled Jane down, since this was only her second ratings period. It is known that Aidn Jones took four years to equal Jane's first rating. In terms of ratings she was successful. There was no reason connected with her program or her performance for Jane to have done better in her first survey than in her second.

How 2GB imagined that Jane would operate optimally in the milieu so quickly is difficult to understand. 2GB was loath to sustain an atmosphere in which she could develop the style and confidence necessary to perfect that media slot, and attract an audience for her more intelligent and involving approach. Yet 2GB had initially recognised the necessity for this, by signing her up on a two-year contract, predicated on the knowledge that it would take her two years to accomplish that end. The Thinking Person's Show would have needed time, and nurturing. It would be a show whose star may have needed a bit for cosseting, and whose audience needed time to acclimatise.

It seems that too many decisions are made on the basis of personality, rather than on professionalism. If there is not a great personal relationship between individuals in the workplace, but there is a strong, productive, professional relationship, then surely that should be sufficient; it should be recognised and stuck to.

Jane's ABC sacking had been a painful treatment, meted out over a long, well-publicised period. It was a 'death of a thousand cuts'.

While she was spreading the Vegemite sandwiches for the children in the faraway Queensland homestead, that phone call from 2GB knifed its way to Jane. The next day's Sydney papers announced: 'Welcome Back, Ms Singleton—You're Fired'.

It was a harsh, commercial decision, fiercely quick.

'It was as if I had died', said Jane, 'and people didn't know what to say'.

On her return from that holiday, Jane went and packed up her office. She was ignored in the hallways. Only Reception offered a self-conscious smile.

One month after her sacking, Jane, the Federal Vice-President of the Australian Journalists' Association, ushered me through the heavy timber door of her and David's rambling, inner-city Victorian house.

Barefooted, soft, very pale-faced, with a new curly hairstyle and summer clothes, Jane led the way down the long central hallway to an airy, sky-lit, blue-ceilinged kitchen which opened on to a series of verandahs surrounded by a mysterious garden that went beyond an unrenovated coach-house in an outer courtyard. There were children's coloured tables and chairs, passionfruits, gardenias, bikes and vines and caves and trees.

Jess and Tommy struggled into the kitchen carrying their little school bags, lunch boxes, and homework books, displaying inordinate curiosity and animation, with shoes whose laces needed tying. There was lots of kissing and smooching and instruction about what needed to happen in the afternoon after school, as David shepherded them into the car and away.

'I'd like to think that if there had not been a series of take-overs while I was there, and had management not been under threat, it wouldn't have happened', said Jane, making a brew of fresh coffee. She was laid back in her domestic mode.

'It was unnecessary to do it on the end of a phone. It could have been done face-to-face. I was not happy to have a phone conversation, which was subsequently misrepresented, and to be in a position of having no come-back'.

Jane's home phone started its regular morning ringing. Her voice was quiet, her manner shy, as she leaned against the kitchen bench. She seemed as though the stuffing had been knocked out of her. She answered each call guardedly. Her maid came in, carrying a tray of wine glasses from last night's dinner party. She shook out the long tapestry cloth to the sparrows in the garden.

'I've made a vow to try and make one call a day asking for a job', Jane said, returning to the verandah table. The flexiglass panels in the roof began to snap and crackle as they expanded in the heat. 'But I find that very, very hard. What am I going to say? "Look, you really need me, I'm terrific"? My stomach gets tied up in knots; I don't have that sort of confidence. Like most women, I'm good at other people's causes. I'd like a husband who'd agree to be my manager—David would be good, he's a farmer, he can sell dead sheep—surely anyone who can sell dead sheep should be able to sell me!'

Though Jane and David battle along like any couple married for fifteen years, Jane is quick to say how much she likes David. She loves knowing that she can return to the centre of her family for a rub-down of soul liniment.

Five years ago, a J. Walter Thompson survey into responses to advertising revealed that the media was aiming its advertisements at women who simply did not exist. The mythical female in suburbia is not sitting out there waiting to be fed on bread and milk. Women listeners are people who live like most of us; they have working lives of some sort or another. They are not particularly concerned with their houses as status symbols. Many are women with active minds who seek effective involvement in the community, or with their children's school, or in the church. Radio station managers seem to forget that their audience is composed of their wives, sisters, daughters and girlfriends. How has the perception persisted that the world of listener-land is different, filled with women who want predictable, sedative radio?

The Sydney *Daily Telegraph* headline on Jane's appointment at 2GB read: 'Jane To Swing Into A Jungle Of Tarzans'. The implication was that her employment at 2GB would help to redress the dreadful imbalance of sexes on Sydney commercial radio. Expectations were stacked on Jane from all quarters. She bit the dust anyway.

Is middle Australia so determined in its poppy-slashing and its mediocrity?

Chris Masters worked beside Jane through the years in Albury, Rockhampton, and now Sydney. He identifies, personally and professionally, with her brand of journalism, with her integrity and with her suffering. He says that he is struck with the recurring thought 'There but for the grace of God go I', as he has watched the rug yanked out from under Jane.

Chris doubts that Jane's sackings have been to do with the fact that she is a woman. He leans towards the belief that it is her brand of journalism, and its delivery, that is the threat. At the same time, he believes that Australian women are more impressive than Australian men, and that the women will ultimately dominate this country. He agrees that this in itself is a threat to the middle Australian male.

Consistent with a theme in the work of his mother, novelist Olga Masters, Chris believes that Australian women discovered themselves in the Depression years, when all of a sudden their men were disarmed. Those hard years built into the women sufficient strength of character for them to carry the weight of the country. They were strong and unrewarded. The men no longer knew how to feed their families; it was the strength of the women that kept food on the table. In the war years, women held the nation's fort, and slowly their unrewarded work became acknowledged.

'I've done a lot of stories about police corruption', said Chris. 'And I've come to the conclusion that there wouldn't be corruption if women were in charge of the police force. By nature, they are closer to understanding injustice—closer to their rage. I can sit down with a group of policemen and say: "Look, this brotherhood syndrome is ridiculous. Why would you support that person? He's a criminal; he sells drugs to children". And they would say: "But he's a mate, you wouldn't understand—this is like a war. He saved my life once!" And the women say: "Bullshit!" Australian women are much more honest. They give decent answers with some sort of sensitivity, and they don't run away from questions. Fifteen years ago I noticed that if I was after the truth, I'd find more of it by asking the women. They are prepared to reveal a little of themselves'.

The Australian media reflect the way men, the power brokers, have controlled women, setting limits on their potential achievements and nit-picking at their performance on all levels of their professionalism.

Is it that there is a large percentage of Australian men who really don't like women? Are they threatened by female power and sexuality? Do they have a parallel fascination with, and horror of, the 'women's business' of giving birth and the mysteries of life that women embody, as they bear the babies and put coins on the eyes of the dead? Is there an element of hatred in the way that some men talk about making love? And do women, in turn, pick up from the masculine culture a degree of self-loathing? The feelings that these questions ignite drift in and out of the consciousness of most of us, and many of us feel fear if we have to define these questions any further, or attempt to answer them.

Australia may be more retrogressive than America. There may be more of a sense of liberty for women in the States. They are reputed to be stronger and more powerful at all levels of public life; yet American media women say they are still pushing up against what they call 'The Glass Ceiling'— the invisible but almost impenetrable barrier that keeps women out of the top levels of management.

Among the women held under the Glass Ceiling are some of the most powerful journalists and editors in this country. It's sad to reflect on the quality of many of the men who sail through to upper management positions, seemingly with little difficulty: for them it's normal career progress, whereas for women to follow the same path is extraordinary, and because it's extraordinary for women to achieve high management positions, stories get written in the media about the women who make it. Those stories, which draw a subliminal distinction between the achievements of women and those of their male counterparts, actually make it harder for women to survive in the positions they have reached by bringing them under a scrutiny in both their private and professional lives that men would not tolerate. It's as if the media were eating its own female babies to ensure the continuation of male supremacy.

In real terms, given the amount of time Jane has worked, what she has done, and the jobs she had held, she ought to be rich and powerful. She is educated, she has a degree, a number of languages, two cadetships; she has worked on some of the best newspapers in the world, and she is respected by some of the best minds in the country.

Women make up 53 per cent of the world's population; they do two-thirds of the world's work; they are paid ten per cent of the world's income, own one per cent of the property; they have the babies, and virtually none of the power. If all things were proportional, 53 per cent of the people in parliament, media corporations, the professions, and the churches would be women.

In such a world, women's ethics, behaviour, intuition, emotions and passions would become part of the norm. Women would no longer be expected to bend or to change to fit into the male mould. Men would merge into the women's template in exchange.

Media women are a linchpin in the move towards a world where truth is not just acceptable but where it is considered a comfortable vehicle for communication. This move is not a matter of ownership, but of attitude; and these women are significant in their contribution to a change in attitude. Media women who are answerable to employers have less opportunity to contribute significantly to a change in attitude on the matter of the truth. Every time one of them bites the dust, a little bit is lost. When Jane falls, and has to weather her period of grief, her grief is on all our heads.

Jane Singleton has an identity despite everything. She is recognised, even if not necessarily by her past employers, by the Australian public as one of our more credible commentators. She will not lose that because she has lost a job.

No doubt there are some aspects of Jane's personality that match the prejudices that are directed against her, whether it be the texture of that personality, her lack of compromise, her highly strung edge, her cultural compassion, her rapid delivery, her defensive insecurities, her commitment to picking out the bones of an issue, her sense of humour, her family ethic, or her refusal to suffer fools gladly.

Jane is as capable of taking on a mangement role as she is of working as a journalist. She is a woman willing to risk all, and obliged to lose all, for excellence in journalism. She is a journalist who in years to come might fly off to any point on the globe and return with surprises—about Gaddafi, Castro or the secrets of the Vatican—that we didn't know we wanted to know until she told us. We would know that she counted it a point of honour to inform us truthfully of the significance.

Ita Buttrose

'I DON'T KNOW WHY I LIKE YOU'

It seems as though the Australian world divides into those who get on with Ita, and like her, and those who don't.

I belong to the admiring mob, who acknowledge the challenge that she presents. I'm curious about where she came from, how she got there and became 'Dame Ita', whence come her energy and drive; and I'm curious about her future, and conscious that maybe she's run off the rails.

The media industry feeds on inspired madness—if it did not Ita might have been selling socks at Myer or living on the Peninsula, majoring in macramé. Hatchet-jobs on her are as common as throw-away lines.

'Who'd be Australian and be a woman?' asks Ita seriously.

'America sees us as Paul Hogan and girls in bikinis. What is the image of a female in this country? The masses watch TV and hope for some clues. There's Olivia Newton-John (born in Britain, resident in the USA). Dame Elisabeth Murdoch, and the Duracks who make up our national female treasures'. Our best-known woman overseas is a man.

The first thing I heard when my arrival was announced by a phone call between two rooms with an open door, was 'Oh, she's early. Have her wait'.

I could hear Ita talking quickly, brightly with the man I had car-tussled with outside in the street. We had jostled for a park; I'd deferred to his aggression, allowing him to take the loading zone, and bided my time for a legitimate space. I climbed the pale grey stairway leading off the discreet city street.

I had not seen Ita for 26 years. That long ago, we had spent a year as colleagues in the rickety old hallways and nooks and crannies of Australian Consolidated Press. We had been cadets together on the *Daily Telegraph*, working for a social editress, racing off at noon with a press photographer to catch the matrons of Sydney sipping sherries before eating mornays at Romano's and Prince's. Or we would be picked up at 4 a.m. by ACP cars, to be driven to the quay and board the press launch to chug out to the Heads, rain or clear dawn, to climb the rope ladders on the waiting liners that plied their way between England and Australia. We were looking for stories. What would we find? A Russian scientist? A violinist? An Auschwitz survivor starting a new life in the sun? We would find gaggles of well-bred twenty year olds returning home after the obligatory European Tour: they would have marriage on their minds, or maybe some sort of working life. Queues of expectant travellers would wait to clear customs as the ship inched its way to its berth.

Ita, Dimity Torbett and I had helped each other with our stories, swapped jobs to suit ourselves and competed in a pretty co-operative sort of way: or so I had thought. But then again, Ita always wanted to be busier.

Her full, curvy body bustled everywhere when we were

girls. The bustling seemed to throw a ring of separateness around her, an efficiency that was very private, and that didn't invite intimacy. The rest of us were swapping insecurities about how tedious cadetship was, and chatter about the wiles of David McNicoll, and wondering why we were not used as 'news' reporters. We were girls. We pulled our hair back into ponytails, and often wore gloves in winter. We ate our first moussaka together at 'The Greeks'.

Ita invented cappucino in the days when there were few migrants, and Lorenzini's was the place to go, for first-year university students, to feel sophisticated with a glass of red wine and thick slices of gouda on crusty rolls. They were the days when nothing seemed bad at all except going back across the street to the musty, overbearing silence of the Mitchell Library.

Ita made her cappucino at the *Daily Telegraph* behind the sticky varnished plywood partition that was our little kitchen in 'social', where we used to hang our coats. There was an old hot water jug and a selection of dismal cups and saucers. We didn't use mugs in those days of the early 60s.

Ita's coffees were a matter of pride. She poured a few drops of boiling water onto the teaspoonfuls of coffee powder and sugar in each cup, then stirred madly until the paste had become so smooth and blended that it had turned almost white. Onto that she poured, all the while stirring briskly, the rest of the boiling water. She would bear these steaming cups out into the office, proud of her wonderful, frothy, hot drinks.

Those were the days when Clyde and Kerry Packer were 'the lads', and Sir Frank was the accessible old shining light of the whole show. Ita's father, Charlie Buttrose, was in high relief in Ita's daily life. His quick step and overseer manner made its mark. His imprint contributed to his daughter's drive for perfectionism, and her confidence.

As the father of a daughter and three sons, Charlie Buttrose, it is said, demanded that they take it in turn to sit next to him at the dinner table, so that he might correct their table manners by clipping them across the ears if they deviated

from his standard. One whack was enough for Ita. She was obedient, and would insist that it wasn't her turn for the trial as often as she could, endeavouring to outwit her old man.

When our boss, Loma McDonald, left for America in 1964, Ita was appointed women's editor of the *Daily Telegraph*. At the tender age of 22, she would come to the door of the copy room, clap her hands and sing out: 'Rally, girls!' By then I was in America. Today, Dimity Torbett recalls: 'I could but gaze balefully at her in a mild state of shock'.

At the age of 35, Ita was appointed editor of the ailing *Women's Weekly*.

It's one thing to see Ita on television. It's another to experience her energy as she walks across the carpet, shoulders back, head high, curvy body seemingly packed with reserved energy.

We greeted each other, taking note of each other's signs of ageing, which subtly told of the different paths our lives had taken in the quarter-century since we had met. Her skin is cared for, her body still full, her jewellery exquisite. She bustled towards me, and a beam of shimmering energy seemed to issue forth from her, across which one could be transported. I know it is one of her methods; it felt like the absolute spontaneity of life-force. We sat facing each other in her unadorned office, with comfy tapestry work chairs and a blue/grey stained wooden desk. Our children made an easy conversational link for us.

Ita was at work, and glamorous. She wore a flowered crepe dress, a purple jewel at her throat, and purple-tint lipstick and nails. She seemed the complete executive. As she was breaking in staff at the same time as she was launching her own Capricorn Publishing and giving birth to *Ita* magazine, I could almost hear the groans of growing pains rippling through the building. They were parallelled by uncertainty, expectation, and excitement at the web of new relationships forming. It felt as though a vow of warriorship might have been demanded of each recruit. Creative austerity and obedience were the order of the day.

'Well, what was I going to do with the next twenty years?' said Ita, whose career past she bears like a bridal train. 'Was I going to stay in the corporate structure as I currently know it? Was I going to look for another opportunity in another corporate structure? No: I know enough to be on my own. The advantage of getting older is that you can have a clearer outline of what is actually achievable. A magazine that says it's o.k. to be older'.

Ita magazine was pitched at the *Cleo* reader who is now seventeen years older. In her way, Ita was answering the archetypal publishing question: do you grow older with your readers? Or do you keep young to attract new readers? Do you break new ground and regain the original readers?

Ita's ambition was to publish a magazine that she herself would be interested to read; that would have a high level of integrity, and which would reflect her own integrity. It would be a vehicle for her love of the world of publishing. Its content would be an expression from her heart of those things she considers valuable, important and relevant for 'the women who wasn't born yesterday'.

To keep her integrity Ita would have let her heart play a part as well as her head; and she would have to be true to her real self rather than just to her ego. The need to be true to our real self is a challenge which hits many of us in middle age, at that time when we look around at our achievements, our home, our grown children, our career, and wonder 'Is this it? Is this all there is?' If up to that point, ego has been our major drive (and human nature insists that it be so for most of those who achieve any sort of 'success'), then there comes time for a change when we confront the yearnings in our hearts for a greater sense of fulfilment, for a greater sense of unity with others, for more spiritual peace.

We can ignore the stabbing voice inside that urges us to make the shift from ego to soul; or we can follow it with the same blaze of determination that we previously demonstrated in achieving material goals, only to find after

months or years of self-transforming study and application that it was still the ego operating to keep us ahead of the pack. Sting sings 'How fragile we are'. How fragile, indeed. We find it hardest to do that which should be quite simple; to lay our egos aside and behave with integrity in our hearts and souls.

How does all this apply to Ita? Only she would know. But in the world of publishing, there are decisions to be made. They can be made on the basis of economic return, or glamour, or conscience, but they have to be made. Whose advertisements will be accepted? Those of planet-rapists and drug dealers such as cigarette companies and breweries? How does one balance ethics and economics? Is it possible to win while running a noble race? How will Ita be remembered by her employers, her employees, her colleagues and her committees? She has twice been voted the 'Most Admired Woman in Australia'. What do Australians most admire? The power to chart one's own course, name terms, call the shots, be quick off the mark; or the grace to concede, to make fertile space for others to grow, to demonstrate compassion and understanding?

Ita is endowed with both of these sets of qualities, as are we all. Which qualities do we expect that she demonstrate most, in order for her to be our 'most admired woman'?

She has also been dubbed 'the most powerful woman in Australia', and has gone through stages of having her sights set on the Prime Ministership. She had controlled five magazines and millions of readers, and has influenced the exchange of many millions of dollars. Now she is chipped away at, by those who believe she has lost that power. Her perceived 'power' of having been a Packer girl, Sir Frank's and Kerry's; of having sought editorial independence from Rupert Murdoch; of 31 years of service to media barons and three years as 'Dr NACAIDS' as she was affectionately called as Chairwoman of the National Committee on AIDS; all this is in her past, as critics are eager to point out. It's as though there is an element of triumph in the writings that say that the power is gone, that Ita is on her last gamble, exposed as a sitting duck for ridicule.

Ita, the woman, has power. It's her nature. She's at a loss to understand why some people make such an issue out of it. If she were as delicate as the jewels at her throat she might wilt; but she's come a long, tough road, and she's more robust than her careful femininity betrays.

Ita, the magazine, may flourish or fall. Either way it will mark a point in publishing history. It will be part of the movie reel called Colourful Ventures: the dreams that became realities, whose lives were long or short, sweet or bitter, remembered by many or merely a few. The vain and the glorious—symbols of where we stood at a given moment. A collection of dreams in which people had the faith to invest money, energy, and love.

Marketing in Australia is well documented, and according to that documentation approximately 85 per cent of all new products launched are failures. What happens to the creators of those failed ventures? Does their personal power die with the change of job, or the change in direction, or the failure of their idea?

Ita has a tangible vitality. Its entry point is her eyes, eyes that she closes for moments on end when she's concentrating, eyes that throughout our time together filled ever so slightly with tears, just a glazing of the blueness when she was talking about something that had hurt.

'I don't want to be owned', she said firmly. 'I want freedom, and what I've been doing is busily getting my freedom. When I worked for Packer, I couldn't go on holidays without his permission. If I went to lunch, they had to know where I was—a ridiculous imposition. What if I had been going down the street to have lunch with a bloke I was in love with? If Kerry was coming home from overseas we were expected to be there, to cancel our own arrangements if he wanted to have an executive lunch upstairs.'

She leaned forward, playing with her black-rimmed glasses. 'I don't want to live or work like that. I just feel there are other things I've got to do'.

By choosing to publish her own magazine, Ita has set herself up to sit again at the table with her father—set up for someone to give her a 'clip on the ear', and to compete with those who had corporate control over her in the past. It's a set-up in which she will be reminded of all the times she was whacked for not meeting with paternal approval.

By attempting to break free, she is aiming for a sense of empowerment. Yet here she is, competing with Kerry Packer, a man who is known to have a spot-on feel for the market. Once there was widespread speculation that she was in love with him. Now she is in competition with the power of his organisation.

Kerry Packer knew just when to buy back his company, Consolidated Press Holdings, part of which is the magazine division of Australian Consolidated Press. He was the first to fight the government and embrace satellite communication. He's always just a step ahead of everyone else. Kerry has developed an extraordinary ability to judge people. He has an infallible memory. He's revered, hated, and respected. He places a high value on loyalty and shows loyalty in return. He's hefty competition for anyone.

Ita magazine's designer was sitting opposite her boss. 'Just take my word for it', said Ita strongly, leaning forward. Then suddenly she yelled towards the door: 'Where's Patsy?'

She yells a lot, speaks loudly and gaily into the phone. She has created an environment where she can be as noisy as she likes.

'No, don't go looking for her', she told the person who was trying to find Patsy. Taking notes, she checked through the folder of the new lay-out while the designer sat waiting for the judgment. Ita is crisp, open, direct. She laughed gustily, taking out a transparency of Paloma Picasso.

'I want to know what it costs . . . ' said Ita.

She and the young designer talked about Paloma's jewellery.

'I don't like this. Where are your headings?' Ita asked. She doesn't waver.

'I'm not going to be able to give you headings ahead of time', said the designer.

'I want to change that', Ita replied. The designer sat quietly. Ita hits and her word is final.

'I had to do a fair bit of work on this copy', Ita went on. She was the epitome of the publisher who is editing. Her black-rimmed glasses came off and went on again. She closed her lips and tucked in her chin to concentrate.

'The *Weekly*'s fashion was wonderful', she told the designer, who was just a baby when Ita was with *Women's Weekly*.

'Black and white is very hip', said the designer.

'This will be 50s and 60s revisited', said Ita. 'I'll have to ask Nan. How lovely the *Weekly* was in its day'. She was turning over old pages. 'Could you get a paste-up of it to me this week?' Dead silence.

'Maybe', said the designer, betrayed by her youthful blushing.

'Maybe?' repeated Ita, with an exquisite blend of sarcasm and humour. 'If I decide to run it', she added, pulling rank. Her eyes twinkled.

The designer blushed more deeply. Ita held her gaze.

'Yes, of course', said the designer, pulling her forthrightness back. She will learn to be creatively productive—and submissive.

A slight edge of impatience shot through the room.

'Come on', said Ita. 'I've got lunch at quarter to one'.

'When people do get through to Ita, and discover there's a real woman underneath who is straightforward and honest, they like her', said Patsy Hollis, a senior journalist and consulting editor for Ita magazine. 'As a boss, she's strong and supportive. She has a strong ego that doesn't get in the way. She is not one to suffer fools. She'll chew you up if you've done something wrong; but having chewed you up and sorted out the mess, that's it. It's not referred to again. She doesn't hold grudges and bring up sneaky little bits in conversation.'

Patsy, as part of the vanguard of freelance journalists, is happy to be a part of the Ita team. She said: 'Ita is naturally powerful, and women don't usually allow themselves to expose who they are. Take away her sex and she's an exceptional business person. I don't think she's trying to be powerful; she just is. It puts her into head-on conflicts with men who can't handle people they see as powerful who happen to be female. I've travelled with her. She goes out of her way not to exert power. She's not gushy. She could be a real queen bee if she wanted to, and she's not. She's accessible and very kind to anyone who comes up to her in the street. She's a great workaholic, takes too much on to her shoulders, and only lets go in small bits, but rarely, because she probably realises that she does it better than anyone else anyway. I've never seen Ita put her ego in the way of her work or the people she's working for'.

Not blatantly, that is. Ita's ego manifests itself as an insistence that she's correct. She has the ability to erode the confidence of somebody she's negotiating with, so that her side of the negotiation is the one that remains. She has exquisite timing, always.

When we set high goals for ourselves, we are empowering

the ego and giving it the feeling that it can do anything. The ego feels nice and powerful and equal to any task. At the same time, it seems that the person is far from being personally empowered, because that person has to step outside the self to see what the end result might be. The power is dependent upon the result. True personal empowerment must lie in expression of the essence of who one is, exactly in the moment of being, not relying on something that will show up later.

Personal empowerment seems synonymous with the energy that manifests through the expression of love. If the love is flowing, and the desire to control is absent, a person is in his personal power, because love is the ultimate energy.

Ita's power appears to be linked to her capacity to love. It seems that she then clouds the feedback for herself, which would give her happiness and fulfilment, by exerting the power of control.

Glimpses of her strong power of loving are what keep us there, attracted to her energy, recognising her love and generosity. Within her vitality, she could be more trusting.

Ita shifted gear in describing for me her last days at Fairfax. Casualties in the Fairfax empire shake-up were much greater than anything that has occurred in publishing in recent times. Two papers died—the *Times on Sunday* and the *Sun*. Many people lost their jobs.

'I wouldn't buckle under, and that's what they wanted me to do', said Ita. 'It made me even more determined to succeed. That's not to say I was not hurt. I will never allow myself to be put into some of the situations I've been in, in my career, ever again. I'm more street-wise now.

'I was at Fairfax from 1984–88. In the beginning I was working at Fairfax magazine. I was publishing consultant for *Woman's Day* and writing for the *Sun*. Well, when Fairfax sold all their magazines to Kerry Packer, I knew I had not been forgiven for leaving all those years earlier, even though I had given 23 years of my best.

'They didn't want me back, and I knew it wasn't going

to be a goer. They shut the *Sun* while I still had a very good contract so I was transferred within the company. I knew Martin Dougherty was going there, and I thought I could work with him. So when they offered me the job of editor-in-chief of the *Sun-Herald*, I thought o.k.! After all, I'd done it before down at Rupert's place. But Martin didn't last very long, so there I was with people I would not have chosen to work with. I was fundamentally a Martin Dougherty appointee, and you've only got to look at the court case to know there was no love lost beweeen Martin Dougherty and the Fairfax management.

'So on the one hand I had Chris Anderson, the editorial executive, writing me notes telling me he thought I was doing a good job; and on the other hand, he came to me one day and told me he didn't think I was going to create the paper he wanted.

'This happened on Friday. He said I should leave that night; I replied: "Not unless you want me to. I'll finish the paper off".

'He said: "I don't know why I like you". Of course, what he was saying was that I was being professional. What kind of behaviour did he expect? I would hope that the least I am is professional.

'I didn't tell anyone—I felt too shocked. I knew it was going to happen sooner or later, but it didn't make the shock any easier to bear. I went to work on Saturday morning. Nobody had told the staff. My replacement knew. It got to be the end of the day, and I wrote my own obituary notice, just two paragraphs. Then I went to tell the staff.

'It was their busiest time. I thanked them. I couldn't talk. There are times when your mouth won't work. I scuttled back to my office. We finished off the paper. A few of them bought me some champagne. At nine o'clock I left.

'That was the end of four and a half years with Fairfax. I went home and still couldn't tell anybody, not even my children'. Ita was telling the story with one arm wrapped around her middle. The other hand with its ringed fingers was held against her throat.

'If I'd made a song and dance, it would have been turned and twisted against me. There's no point in adding fuel to the fire. If you're well-known in Australia, you'll get it. It's such a tough business for women.

'When I got to Rupert's, I was editor-in-chief of two *Teles* in 1980. Then I became editor-in-chief of the *Sun-Herald* in 1984. No other woman had come along; that's because women know how tough it is—they actually know. Unless a woman is as stubborn and as determined as I am to get on, few women will put up their hands and go for it. It's so hard to take the knocks.

'I can't help it if I'm confident and forthright. Why should I play dumb? Some man said to me the other day that men wouldn't get heart attacks if they had wives who weren't very well educated and who were basically stupid. What sort of garbage is that? Women should be stupid so men won't have heart attacks?

'If Jane Singleton had been a man, she would have been treated far more kindly. Who's going to try commercial radio after seeing the treatment she got?

'When Margaret Thatcher was here, the media was obsessed with her hair because it didn't blow out of place. She doesn't look any good if her hair is blowing everywhere—of course she's going to have it lacquered into place. Surely on a windy day Bob would have a bit of lacquer on his hair. Thatcher's not an 18 year old roaming around in an MG—she's the leader of a nation. Nothing will change so long as the textbooks imply that the boys are the doers and the girls are not'.

To launch a magazine in the cold world of publishing, Ita hoped that she would no longer be at the mercy of her bosses. She thought that, by running her own company, she could be free of corporate patriarchs. The goal of getting free is different from the goal of running a successful magazine.

We're truly powerful only when we're not secretly proving something to someone, which is giving away power to another person who might be making an assessment. Ita has mastered the art of approval-seeking, as is demonstrated by her two 'Most Admired Women' awards. But she's also had her share of being a victim of the famous Australian 'tall poppy' syndrome, of the relentless chopping that tends to befall those who attain a high profile.

Kerry Packer had given Ita a setting where she looked as though she had power; but the setting was a straitjacket of imposed social consciousness, ensuring that she stayed bound. Her models were the women of the 50s and early 60s—Nola Dekyvere and her ilk, the hardworking maverick female journalists like Mrs Fenston, Nan Musgrove, and Mary Coles.

Perhaps while emulating the excellence of these female media pioneers, Ita had overlooked her more contemporary sisters in today's world of communications; the ones who were looking into other levels of consciousness and taking a more holistic approach to the way they reflected the community back to itself. She now says that she wants Julie Clarke working for her, which indicates that the Richard Neville/Julie Clarke school of contemporary commentary hovers in the background for her with its unashamed agenda of speaking about our responsibility to the soul of who we are. That's a long way from the white-gloved, straight-seamed, perfectly groomed-with-a-saucy-hat style of three decades ago.

'You have no idea of the hurt in Ita', said Nan Musgrove, now in her seventies and still a prolific writer. 'No one knows Ita who only knows her publicly. I've never known anyone so compassionate and warm'.

Nan Musgrove is Ita's friend, mentor, and now employee. Nan was the first woman journalist in the Australian Press Gallery at Parliament House, in John Curtin's time. She was a crack shorthand writer, and a second-year cadet who had never seen a politician. In those days she was told she was not to use the Parliamentary common room. 'I did anyway, and they looked the other way', she said, sparkling with mirth at the memory of her wickedness. John Curtin, as Prime Minister, would unobtrusively protect Nan in the Gallery. If someone jumped ahead of her, he would quickly interject with 'Ladies first!'; or he'd greet her in a room full of men and single her out by saying: 'And Miss Musgrove, what have you on your plate today?'

Ita has drawn on Nan's example for thirty years. She loves and trusts her.

'You don't get where Ita's got on the "lay-by",' said Nan severely, 'in other words, lying back for some man or men. She's proved over and over again how capable she is on her own merit.'

This was clearly intended as an answer to criticisms of the way in which Ita has conducted her career.

'It's the pressures on Ita that have created her. One of the things that irks Ita's critics', Nan continued, 'is how she always looks. Some women will say, "Oh, she can afford to—look at the money she makes." But when Ita was fifteen she was like that. She'd do her nails on the bus. When she was young she would never move into the public arena without first giving her dress or blouse the once-over with the iron. In her office at Consolidated Press she always had an ironing board. Even if she was going out to lunch with just me', said Nan with an edge of incredulity, 'she'd be in there pressing the bow on her blouse. I've seen her when she was Dr NACAIDS, noticing a spot on her white jacket and getting out the old dry-cleaning fluid. Whatever she has is as good as she can make it. I think she's got a dynamo in her. She's determined, she's ambitious, and she knows she has the energy to meet whatever demands she makes on herself.'

'What drives her, Nan?'

'She's always wanted to be her own person. She doesn't want to be dependent on anyone. She saw her parents' marriage break up; she saw her mother's lack of independence. As the only girl with three brothers, she was always the little mother. Her brothers are all volatile. Ita has a half Jewish grandmother from whom she's inherited passion, drive and intelligence. She is influenced by her grandmother—her bearing, her proud walk and her deep sense of privacy'.

I remembered the blue in Ita's eyes changing colour when she gazed out of the window next to her desk and told me of the last days at Fairfax. Her discipline overcomes any hurt more than adequately. Unless one is able to sit quietly with

Ita, one could miss the subtle changes that come over her when she touches on the areas of pain throughout her life.

Nan Musgrove says that Ita has been a tremendous influence in her life. Twenty-five years Ita's senior, Nan is comfortable in her high-rise living room, looking out over the water. Dressed in a brightly printed, loose summer dress, hair piled high on her head, there is an air of elegance about her. Her intuitive understanding of Ita stems from her deep love for her. Ita could be her daughter: in fact, she's Nan's boss.

'I was at the *Weekly* for years', said Nan. 'Down there in a corner doing my pages about television, interviewing celebrities. In 1975 Kerry moved Ita down to us. Dorothy Drain had retired, for which Ita got the blame. So Ita came into an atmosphere of mistrust and blame, apprehension and unfriendliness. It was an awful beginning. Lots of people didn't like her'.

Nan was working on a medical project that needed one hundred questions asked about First Aid. Nan begged Mrs Fenton for some help with her research. It was a Friday, and she was surrounded by books from the St John's Ambulance Brigade. It was then in 1958 that Ita, as a fifteen year old, first came to Nan's attention when Mrs Fenton said: 'Look, I've got a very bright copy girl. You know her, Ita Buttrose, she gets the tea. I think she could help you'.

So Nan got hold of Ita, who arrived on the Monday having worked all weekend. She had done fifty of the questions, and said to Nan: 'I've given you an extra twenty-five in case you don't agree with the ones I've chosen'. All beautifully typed.

'She's always had the makings of a champion. She's always prepared to run that extra half mile', said Nan. 'She used to make tea and coffee for us. The girl before her used to just rinse the cups and stand them upside down on a piece of plastic. Ita used to bring in a fresh tea towel each day, all washed and ironed. She'd do the tea with such care. It's part of her grooming. She can make a treat of anything. She's like a celebration. She's a festive person'.

'It's a celebration of being an older woman—that sort of

feeling'. Ita was trying to describe her vision for *Ita* magazine to the commercial photographer she had chosen to shoot an image of her for the cover.

She has to work hard for an even ride with the boys. Sometimes she becomes one of them. While being super-attractive and proud of her femininity, there are times when she is prepared to sling off even when the topic is not so comfortable for her. She keeps the atmosphere buoyant. She manages to keep a mixed-sex group in one of those heavy-lidded laughs that go on and on until everyone has finished with the mirth inside themselves and they're all watching each other's faces to know when it's o.k. to stop the effort of making believe the joke is still funny. Commanding such a performance serves to add another subliminal layer of armour.

'You mean those older women who still want to look fantastic?' asked the gold-plated photographer.

'Of course,' said Ita, holding back laughter, covering her nerves and intelligence with glamour and wit. Her make-up man was holding her head, brushing her hair back, comforting her with a pat on the knee, sculpting her face and little by little bringing forward the woman that everyone expects.

'Perhaps not blasting it all out', said the young designer of *Ita* magazine directly to the photographer, not wanting to lose the real person.

'On the other hand, though', said Ita with a steely tone that drew everyone's concentration, 'don't show all the wrinkles'.

'Yes, I know I could give you heavy realism,' said the photographer, being too clever.

'Oh God!' said Ita, in recognition of herself.

Ita has worked flat-out as a journalist, editor, columnist, public figure, and community person for thirty-five years straight. She's married and divorced twice, single parented, and single-handedly provided for her children.

'I don't think I've forfeited anything in the pursuit of success', said Ita. 'People see success in such funny ways, don't they? They think of it as sacrifice. To be successful you might have to work hard and not go out, but that's not necessarily a sacrifice if you're enjoying the things you're doing. When I'm too busy and very stretched, I wake up and think I can't wait to come home tonight and go to bed. Sometimes in a lazy morning after my walk, I'll have a bath with oils'.

I wondered whether Ita might not have been happier trying her skills in a new arena, leaving the symbolic 'clip-over-the-ears' table, and maybe opening a lingerie shop.

'I'm told that because I'm a powerful woman, I frighten men,' she said, as we wove our way through city traffic for her to be filmed at the Sydney Town Hall, introducing the Tourism Industry Awards.

'When I was a little girl', she continued, 'I would query things about religion, and the nuns would tell me it was "a mystery", and that I would find out the answer when I died. I hope I find out why men find powerful women threatening before I die!' She laughed.

'I find powerful men really exciting. I like the way their minds work. I like the breadth of their vision. Why they find us threatening beats me. John Singleton reckons we'll never make it because we're not bastards enough. He says we're too honest. Perhaps our openness is misconstrued.

'I'd like to explore these sorts of things in the magazine. Nobody talks about sex properly. We're all hung up about it. If you're honest about it, good love-making is terrific. You sleep well. You can wake up in the middle of the night and do it all over again and it's hot and sweaty and wonderful'. She paused. 'I'd rather not have a sex life than have a rotten one. I couldn't be bothered pretending any more, and you know you can still feel lusty in your seventies. The difference between writing about sex in *Cleo* and in *Ita* magazine will be talking about whether men getting into their fifties can satisfy their women. Older women have to put up with sloppy, inadequate performances a lot of the time. A lot of men know nothing about foreplay. What have they been doing all their lives?'

Ita is loud and full-on when she's relaxed. She's got a wild streak when she waxes forth, and she's lusty.

'I don't know if I want a man', she continued. 'An ideal middle age, if you're not married, would be three days a week; and it's no good having anybody if he isn't good in bed. I get asked to all these wonderful events and parties: I usually go on my own. It would be very nice to go with somebody I knew. Of course, it wouldn't work if he was bored in my settings. The awful thing is that men and women try to change each other. I know that if anyone came along, he would have to take me as I am. Well, if he's attracted to me in the first place, why would he want to change me? But there may be nobody for me, and I accept that.

'I know that I am criticised for being the way that I am. The only way I can cope with the rubbish that is dealt out about me, is with the knowledge that the average person in Australia doesn't see me that way'.

'Will you write for *Ita* magazine like you're speaking to me, Ita?'

'I am untapped. I know I can teach people to be braver about what is truly important', she replied calmly.

For thirteen years, Ita wrote a column every week, encouraged by her cash-register bosses to tell the tales of Kate and Ben. She's ready to push some boundaries: 'I think I am going to become more outspoken. It isn't so easy for a lot of my sisters. Now I have the freedom to push the parameters a bit. I would like to push the boundaries of philosophical discussion for women, particularly'.

Ita's optimism emanates from the essence of who she is. She wouldn't have been able to do what she has done unless she had tremendous spiritual strength. The misdirected part of Ita's power, that prevents her from fully enjoying a sense of fulfilment and happiness, is that she seems not to have connected her personal power to her spiritual self.

She continues to derive her happiness essentially from her children, and her deep sense of humanity is directed towards them. With them, she is totally free to express the power of her love. 'Yes, the children,' Ita said. 'But they're not going to be there forever, you see. You hope that you'll have a relationship that will last. I hope they'll come back to me'.

Few mature women would not identify with the poignancy of that wish, and the soft glazing of Ita's eyes as she expressed it. 'I hope that they'll love me—and that I can still yell at them! Basically, they are my big happiness in life. I work really hard for them. I try to give them a really good life. I went to several schools, and I've worked my butt off to make sure they only went to one. We've worked together for them to be private and not recognised. When Ben monsters me, which I love, I say to him I can't help it, this is me, I'm your mother and that's it'.

So close have the three been across the years that when she was much younger, Kate said to Ita: 'Mum, if you died, would I have to be editor of the *Weekly*?'

Kate is studying architecture, and looks like her father. Ben is finishing school. He's tall and golden and looks like his mum.

'In the end', said Ita Buttrose, 'it's just a matter of when you get up in the morning, do you like what you see?

'And I do!'

Caroline Jones

'HER SEARCH FOR MEANING'

'Never mind paying your dues—everyone's a writer or broadcaster these days'. This was sharp sarcasm from the normally mild-mannered Caroline Jones, the aristocrat of Australian broadcasting. Caroline knows what it takes to be a consummate professional after a quarter of a century in Australian radio and television.

Caroline Jones is 52, and a household name. She is slim as a greyhound, and tough as tempered steel, with a gentleness and sensitivity that increases with age. She is a woman who acknowledges that it was her loneliness and vulnerability which set her on a spiritual path she has incorporated into her career.

Today Caroline is the creator, interviewer and presenter

of ABC Radio National's program *A Search For Meaning*. With this program, Caroline has effected a smooth transition from hard-hitting journalism to a niche that is compatible with her personal development.

Caroline, an only child, describes herself as 'a poor little thing at the Gosford High School' who graduated with four A's and two B's, and dreamed of doing physiotherapy at Sydney University. Instead, she studied at the University of New England in Armidale and was, from the point of view of her country-bred fellow students, 'one of the sophisticated city ones who dated teachers'.

In 1963 Caroline landed herself a job as a part-time presenter and 'jill-of-all-trades' at Channel 3 in Canberra, and her appetite for the theatrical world of the media was thoroughly titillated in those first dizzy days of Australian television. Those were the days when her idol was John Freeman from the 'Face to Face' series.

'Caroline is a very strong person. She was an absolute pioneer on radio and television', said one of her earliest workmates, the presenter of ABC Radio's *PM* program, Paul Murphy. 'She is a natural performer, a natural journalist with natural histrionic talents. She can be devastatingly funny, with one of the sharpest tongues, and when she's relaxing she's a knock-out funny woman'.

The fact that she was a very funny woman helped Caroline's early career in the 60s, when television was a male preserve. She had a tongue that men feared while at the same time falling for her because she was witty and tart.

Sydney's ABC television recognised Caroline's talent and recruited her for *This Day Tonight*. She was the first woman reporter on the team from its inception in 1968. It was during this year that Caroline's mother's death occurred. Caroline doesn't baulk at the explanation that her energy over the succeeding years was driven by her grief at the tragedy of her mother's suicide.

'It was very lonely really', said Caroline. 'My Dad has always been there, and by his presence he has given me great strength. During those years my deep feelings of loneliness were always accompanied by a little voice that said: "How dare you feel so sad, you've got this wonderful job . . . ".'

Caroline Jones did astonishingly good work as a reporter and presenter in her next job, which was as compere of the national current affairs program *Four Corners*. As well as knowing when to go for the jugular, which she did every weekday for some years on *This Day Tonight*, she was good at extracting information and elucidating it for the viewers.

Her stint with *Four Corners* from 1972 to 1981 was the longest compering job that has been held in this country. As well as that, from 1977 to 1981 she brought *City Extra* on radio every morning into the lives of isolated Australian women in suburbia. With these programs she went right to the heart of communication via mass media. She was the listener's mouthpiece, able to ask questions that the average person wanted to ask, while allowing her guests the freedom to be themselves.

Caroline's audience responded in two ways. They felt as though they were being stimulated to think—and they fell in love with Caroline. People felt that if they could sit down with her, they would like her. There was no Caroline view, or Caroline imprimatur. She wasn't on about left, or right, or theistic or atheistic. She was a facilitator. Her object was always to present the balanced picture. This objectivity is seen by her present-day critics as detracting from the excellence of her work.

'In childhood and adolescence I was timid almost to the point of being anaesthetised', said Caroline. 'Out of my immense timidity and shyness I found the gall to ask questions and develop an interviewing style. By the time I was in my mid-twenties, I was divorced and setting upon this career'. She patted the steering wheel of her brand new, sporty little white car. She is not materialistic, and still a bit in awe at choosing a car off the showroom floor. We were heading along the freeway into Sydney's western suburbs, to a Catholic church hall where Caroline was to appear 'live' to another generation of isolated women.

'I've been given so many opportunities. I think that's why

I have this rather burning loyalty to the ABC. It's through the ABC that we've learned about ourselves and about other Australians, about literature, about music, about the world we live in. It's our main forum and teaching instrument. It's terribly important in a country that is so vast, with such contrasts of lifestyle. The ABC deepens our sense of belonging here and being part of a nation. That's why I hang in there, even though they pay only about half the money that would come from anywhere else'.

Caroline never forgets to direct her energy and focus on the whole of Australia. She constantly thinks in terms of what will affect the national listener.

She had been waiting outside in the street for me when I had arrived at 6.30 in the morning, so that I would know I had come to the right place. This element of respect and grace is apparent in each of Caroline's moves. She was welcoming. Her makeup was impeccable, her clothes incredibly stylish, if slightly daunting initially. She was prepared for her coming appearance. I followed her into her apartment. From the front entrance, her soft furniture looked as though it was sitting on top of the harbour. The glass of the windows went down to the floor, so the carpet extended out to a stretch of shimmering blue water. Her bathroom was filled with delicate ferns.

'Have a quick look at my place before we leave'. She was willing to reveal a secret or two. The one that caught my eye was a photograph of her by Peter Solness, thumb-tacked to one of the doors. It was an image of a strong, emotional, almost raunchy, beautiful woman. Peter had caught a moment that I knew I would search for.

'Maybe such loneliness was a positive thing for me', said Caroline as she drove towards the church. 'It kept me reaching out. If you're happy, complacent and content, you can sit like a suet pudding. I contend now (since I am very wise now)', she added, with a wink, 'that loneliness is a boon because it keeps you looking, to make new contacts, to explore'.

Caroline was driving smoothly. We were in the middle lane, like the middle path she has chosen. With her work and her apartment she has insulated herself against the pain of that great personal tragedy—her aloneness. Caroline has been on a long search. With her program *A Search For Meaning* she is publicly encouraging the quest in us all. That has become her personal and professional goal. She has 'gone public' with her own search, and with the nature of her private life.

In her heydey, Caroline was loved by tens of thousands of Australians. In a year when she compered *Four Corners* without doing any reporting she received an award as the most outstanding woman on television. That award was the result of enormous affection. The public love that was directed towards her was her consolation. She was not experiencing the love personally in the way that makes a star inaccessible to the individual. The paradox was that she was being simultaneously fed and sapped by her life with the ABC. In those days it had become her nurture and her deprivation.

Caroline's professionalism is her armour. It is her code, by which people can relate to her, engage and exchange with her. The rules are there, defined and easily translatable. This is the woman who came back to me the next day and told me that she hadn't been truthful in saying that she didn't regret being childless. She would have loved a child. She would have loved to have had one as late as her fortieth year.

'I chose to not be in a relationship that would give me a child', she said. 'I know that I chose that. I can't be too happy with the notion that we create our own reality because that leaves God out of it—the transcendent element in one's life. I don't see myself as the measure of all things, but I do agree that we have free will and get to make choices. To have had a child would have been the ultimate creativity!'

She checked her watch. There were paddocks beside the freeway now, breaks in the landscape before we hit the satellite suburb where forty women would be stashing their preschoolers in the church creche, sucking in their tummies and smoothing down the fabric of their jeans and skirts. They would be arranging the plastic chairs in a wide circle inside the church hall, in readiness for the arrival of their guest speaker, chosen by their parish priest.

Caroline has maintained a high profile in this country. In the process she relinquished her own personal development. Over many years she forfeited the intensity of sexual and non-sexual relationships in order to keep her attention and energy focused on her job.

'I fell in love over the years', she said, 'and always I gave more energy and priority to my work. That energy was born of my unresolved personal life. One's insight into oneself only dawns over periods of years'.

Caroline flipped the car radio on to Radio National. We both listened to the voice of the woman I was interviewing, who was interviewing Ann Fairbairn, translator of Arabic poetry, about her new book.

Caroline's tone of voice changed as we talked about the interview. She seemed to have woven herself back into her professional mesh neatly, like the splicing and joining of a rope.

It felt to me as if we were in the first few minutes of

the movie *Walkabout*, where the radio, sitting on the kitchen bench, with blue water visible through the window behind, churns out a totally familiar ABC piece, nailing the film as indisputedly Australian. Caroline Jones's voice has the same effect. For the years that all of us in our 40s and 50s have been deepening into adulthood, our unconscious has been reassured by the tone of that one particular female voice. Caroline is an institution.

Her profile was sharp against the car's side window, her chin pointy, her hair soft. She was eating an apple quarter that I had peeled for her. Her striped blouse had a high, white, clerical collar. She was keeping to 80 kilometres per hour in a 110 kilometre per hour zone.

'I don't know if I had a nervous breakdown', she said, referring to her collapse and withdrawal from the ABC in 1981. 'It may be described as that. I got very, very tired, and started to become anxious that current affairs programming was contributing to people's anxiety in general. My conscience started to worry me. I knew that loneliness was my real illness. I was terribly lonely. It just grew upon me, and I think it was because I was working that hard and I was single. It might have been different if I could have gone home and shared what was on my mind each night'. Caroline's eyes were wide, her wrists very tiny, as she steered the car.

'I can remember Geraldine (Doogue) saying to me once: "Oh, it's so wonderful to go home at night and talk things over", and I thought gosh, that must be terrific'.

Caroline explained that she started to feel fragmented. She could see who Caroline Jones, the worker, was, but began to lose sight of who was there inside. 'I think that's fairly common with people who have a high public profile', she said. 'I needed to disappear. I needed to have a look within. When I looked, it was terrifying'.

She faced me squarely for a second. Her vulnerability was tangible, yet I imagined that there would never be anything I could do to make her more comfortable.

'I realised why I had kept myself so busy', she said.

'Workaholics don't want to look at the scary side of who they are. Surely our central task is confronting who we are—don't you think? It's our central yearning, isn't it?'

Caroline emanates warmth, yet I felt there was always something in reserve, and what I was getting may not truly have been the rich kernel of what she could offer.

'My walking away from my job was inexplicable—a mystery to a lot of people. Who walks away from an apparently successful situation in the media? I was puzzled and angry. I have always had a much stronger sense of my connection with the audience than with anyone I work with. Somehow I was taking them with me'.

Despite her illness, Caroline remained committed to her ideal of communication as an art form. At that point she was attracted to Hugh Mackay's material in the *National Times*, and invited him to discuss some of his ideas on radio. Hugh is the founder of the Centre for Communication Studies at Bathurst. Subsequently he and Caroline embarked on a series of programs that explored communication skills and conflict resolution techniques.

Hugh recognised Caroline's need for intimacy and rest, and invited her to come to live and work in Bathurst. She limped into the country, tired, disoriented, exploited and genuinely searching. She went as an only child, invited to spend a year in the bosom of Hugh's family with his wife, his newborn child, and his mother. Caroline speaks of that period with love. Within a nurturing environment she blossomed and expanded slowly beyond the intellectual limitation that was part and parcel of her job at the ABC. She added a high profile to Hugh's operation, and became skilful in dealing with small groups, extending the way she had worked in radio.

She began to see the facilitating role as a precious one in the community—to see that the essence of communication is that one commits oneself to understanding the capacities and dispositions of the 'other', the audience; and to see that other people will respond to you because you have first responded to them.

Caroline's great gift as a public person was her capacity

to listen. Hugh Mackay describes the 'listening' process, by first explaining that we are caged by our prejudices, our values, our attitudes, our beliefs, and the fruits of our experience— these become the bars of our cage. We don't see the world as it is, we see the world with the template of our prejudice imposed on it. 'When we listen, really listen', Hugh said, 'we step outside that, and step into the cage of the other. We try to feel it as they feel it, and see it as they see it'.

Hugh Mackay says that Caroline's public performance was one in which she did that beautifully; but he added that privately, she had great difficulty in doing it. Caroline became exhausted by the inherent commitment at Bathurst to 'communicate' in personal and private relationships. She became critical of the emphasis on sensitivity in communication. She was impatient with Hugh. Her own search for meaning was under way.

She moved through a series of self-transforming workshops and seminars in an effort to shed her pattern of aloneness. Her effort was to express the love of who she is, beyond simulating it as a communicator. She wanted loving contact; she wanted to cut through her isolation. Caroline was at ease when speaking of this period of her life. It is the sort of material she elicits from her interviewees, her way of making herself feel safe. It's the same safety she offers her interviewees when she steers clear of challenging them.

'Through personal development courses, I found great relief from feeling separate', she said. 'I had felt embattled and alone so often before, and as though I had to be in control of it all'.

Caroline turned the car off the freeway into a wilderness of newly tarred suburban streets. It was hot and dry; the sky was brown. Blasts of dust blew into the air. The bushes and trees in the housing tract were small, where there were any at all. There were no developed gardens: the soil wasn't ready after the bulldozers had razed the paddocks. The subdivision houses hadn't settled on to their foundations yet.

'It was so lonely to take the whole world on to one's shoulders', she continued. 'I don't think that's how we're meant to be as human beings. Through the intimacy of the courses, I was able to feel a personal connection with people. Those courses opened me up to new possibilities. One of those was the finding of a "home" in the Catholic way of understanding the mysteries'.

We pulled to a standstill in the rippling heat of the church's asphalt parking lot. Everything was glaring. Caroline was questioning herself as we sat there quietly. 'Who am I to go in and tell these women anything? After all, they are the ones shouldering the huge responsibilities of life, and doing things that really matter', she said.

We sat watching the women mill around the church hall door. Women, many of them, who had finally mustered the energy and assertion to eject husbands who had been getting drunk and beating them and not coming home to the little residence they were paying off. Many of these women were single parents. Their psyches were as uncomfortable with the landscape as the little houses perched on it.

These women were getting to know each other under the umbrella of the Catholic Church. They had come to hear Caroline, the radio star they listened to for inspiration throughout the week.

The parish priest and his visiting locum, Father Paul Coleman, greeted Caroline with demonstrative affection. One rested his hand protectively on her thin shoulder and ushered her into the group. A florist's arrangement marked her chair.

'Caroline's wonderful. We listen to her all the time', the women next to me leaned over and whispered.

Perhaps twenty years of ABC training had readied Caroline for the strictures of Catholicism. Her big eyes circled the women, expressing the great need within her to make contact. I found myself wondering whether John Gorton, on her show, had explained the most telling moment about his scarred face because Caroline's eyes had beckoned with their particular need.

Alexander Lowen, in *The Language of the Body*, borrows a theme from Reich to describe the 'oral' personality. Where Reich had likened this adult type to a baby which constantly searches for its mother's nipple, but remains insatiable no matter how much nourishment it gets, Lowen adds a 'body type' to the picture and says that the 'oral' personality is typically tall and thin, with very big eyes which search for nourishment just as actively as does their mouth. Perhaps it is Caroline's 'orality' which calls upon and draws out the softness and truthfulness within each of her interviewees.

The women listened carefully. Some started gently to kick their sandals off their stockinged feet. Caroline was approachable as she talked about her own anxiety. She was tutoring them to recognise more about themselves. 'We can be fully alive about what's happening right now', she said cheerfully, 'not what's happening at work, or how it will be for Billy in the dentist's chair'.

The women in the audience smiled, and recrossed their legs.

'I'm not wanting to be glamorous or foolish about this', Caroline said. 'I'll just read a little poem and we'll do something together'.

She read from *The Prophet*. There was a droning, downbeat feeling. Perhaps it was my personal reaction to the effect of seeing good Catholic girls toeing the line. They are used to sitting still for the sermon, yet this preacher was saying 'stay in the present', and speaking of Zen Buddhism. Women self-consciously sneezed into their tissues. The air-conditioning was turned on full.

'The perfectionist is not a compassionate person', said Caroline. I had lost the thread of this part, and was not sure to whom she was referring.

Afterwards, Caroline circulated among the women as they ate their sandwiches in the courtyard. They waited their turn to chat and ask advice.

Father Paul Coleman was firm as he pressed his invitation on Caroline and me to have a prepared lunch in the priest's dining room. We were served sizzling schnitzel by a punk girl with gelled hair and black clothes. Father Coleman had spent the previous day counselling and hearing confessions at one of the maximum security prisons. He was feeling saddened by the overcrowding in New South Wales jails, and was reflecting on the counter-productive aspects of imprisoning all the state's car thieves. I moved into the discussion with equal vehemence. Caroline sat back, looking vague and beautiful with a sort of iridescence—shimmering, but only just hovering on the edge of being at one with her soul.

Caroline gets much of her intellectual and personal nourishment from Paul Coleman. He is an effective man, witty and sarcastic, worldly, warm, and a dedicated Jesuit. He has a sort of 50s way of saying something risqué, and then giving the likes of me a nudge and a wink.

Paul Coleman stepped into Caroline's life when not only her career, but even her search, had come to a halt. She was experiencing vulnerability, having left Hugh Mackay's orbit, and the alienation that comes from being a perfectionist and a formal communicator. At that time in her life, Caroline was invited by the organisers of an ecumenical gathering in the Catholic church at North Sydney to present the Christmas liturgy.

She liked the liturgy. She liked what she saw, and heard, and experienced. One evening she went up to Paul Coleman in the churchyard and asked him to teach her about the church. The next Monday at 10 a.m. Caroline was to embrace what she calls her 'new grid, new framework, new support'.

'She was in an emotional desert', said Father Paul. 'She had to find her way through a series of relationships, and one of the final relationships was with the Catholic community. She was prepared to open herself to peace and let God speak to her. It was not just the mechanics of the Church that attracted her. It was the spirit of God that's within Caroline that was beginning to manifest itself', he said.

Caroline's book, *The Search For Meaning*, describes her entry into the Church: 'There followed a number of conversations over many months, with two priests separately, who seemed able to discern the yearning child within the public figure. I knew that wisdom, acceptance, gentleness and generous accessibility, the listening of these two men, were signs of God. It was like falling in love; irrational, but irresistible'.

'It's easy for me to be close loving friends with Paul, because I know the limitation of it', Caroline told me, as we wended our way back to the heart of Sydney. 'I think in friendships between men and women the sexuality is always there, because there is always that "zing", but if a friend has chosen a celibate way of life, then that is very clear. These new friendships are very important for me, because I am single. Of course, they must be to everyone, because you can be lonely in a marriage'.

The Church for Caroline is like a homecoming. It is the womb, the family, the home. Since her baptism, she acknowledges that she is giving and receiving more warmth and intimacy than at any other stage in her life.

Caroline is criticised by some, within and outside the media, who are disappointed that their pin-up girl has become a 'flake'; that the ABC is funding what some call 'The Catholic Hour'.

Caroline isn't religious in the narrow sense. She is interested in religion to the degree that she recognises that there is a dimension to existence other than the mechanistic and materialistic elements of human life. She is using religion as a springboard for a broader look at life.

The key is her willingness to listen. In her radio program, she has created the role of the non-judgmental 'active listener' as she draws from her interviewees their stories, peeling away layers of their experience to find whatever religious or spiritual insights may be there giving meaning to their lives. To allow someone to tell their story without imposing one's viewpoint requires tolerance and openness; Caroline has to be as open with her subjects as they are with her. This demands an inner strength from her, and a preparedness to be vulnerable.

This breaks one of the rules of good radio, in which there is an expectation that the broadcaster will to some degree act as a representative of the audience, and ask the questions the audience would ask, even if there is judgment implicit in the questions. Being determinedly gentle, Caroline is open to the criticism that her program is too saccharine, and that she herself is a fence-sitter.

This is exemplified for me when I asked her whether she

had 'believed' some of the remarks made by Aboriginal activist Burnum Burnum in her interview with him: 'Oh!' she said, surprised. 'I've never really thought about that, whether I do or not'.

She avoids judging the material that she extracts from her subjects to the extent, apparently, that it's immaterial whether what they tell her is true. Her only aim is to get them to open up. Some of them may be quite fraudulent in their expositions of the 'deep and meaningful' in their lives, but even within these, Caroline would say, there are spiritual dimensions to be explored.

Caroline's boss, David Milliken, is a Christian theologian who heads the religious department of the ABC. He believes that this aspect of her personality is Caroline's greatest strength.

'Her professionalism is driven by a type of humanness, a desire for contact with her audience, that she exemplifies by writing all her own letters. Her manner flies in the face of the cavalier attitude of the media that sees the audience simply as fodder', David said. 'It's an attitude that says if the audience likes you, that's fine, but you don't have to respect them or like them; if they are there in great numbers you are successful, and they are wonderful; if they're not there with you, you try to make adjustments and get them back again. Caroline gives the impression that she is speaking to a huge range of people with whom she genuinely wants to communicate. She has the need to be liked and loved, and people know that'.

Caroline believes that *The Search For Meaning* is exempt from criticism in the same way that religion is beyond the adversary process of the law. She believes that her program is getting down to what really matters about human life, and that the program acts as a salve to heal society as people wake up to their own humanity and find a wellspring of love and compassion for one another. That's best accomplished in a non-judgmental atmosphere.

Her critics claim that now she has the guiding structure of Catholicism in her life she lays it over whatever new information she is about to process. They argue that this lessens the program as a true quest or search. They claim that if we listen to the enthusiasm with which she responds to the religious answer, we will notice too that there is a caution and a sceptical tone when she obtains the non-religious answer. Some say that she now has her path, and that she's leading others up it to comment on the flowers that she has planted, bringing about a uniformity and a lack of challenge both for herself and for her subjects.

Radio is subtle, and radio audiences have increased in proportion to the fragmenting of Australian society. Almost half the houses in Sydney contain only one or two people— 27 per cent of Sydney homes contain only one person. And we are moving towards an increasingly aged population. Radio is a voice around the house, a constant companion. No other medium gives such a sense of one-to-one communication.

In the area of religion, people from both sides of any issue will hear what they want to hear. Good radio is when people react, whether positively or negatively. If a listener is wandering around the house muttering 'Rubbish!' it doesn't necessarily mean he is panning the program. It's more likely to mean that it's a good program even though he disagrees with the ideas he is hearing. He is still involved, and stimulated.

Of Caroline's critics, Father Paul Coleman says: 'They are facile spinners of words. They want to say she has lost her professional edge. But she is exploring new ground. She is trying to come to terms with human alienation and a spiritual malaise that is hitting the world. There are those who say that professionally she is lost; but the public, whom she is touching, says, "we need you". They may be the middle-aged and older, who are in the most need of unlocking their spirituality. They may have been good at their jobs, but perhaps deep down they are conscious of an emptiness in their lives'.

Caroline considers herself to be a revolutionary. 'If I'm not, then I'm wasting my time', she said. 'I am revolutionary in that I have little faith in the political process from my observation of it, and I believe that the way to make the necessary changes in our society is for people to wake up on an individual level, and hear each other. The connections need to be made at a grass-roots level. There are tremendous divisions in this country between classes and degrees of affluence, backgrounds and races. One of the greatest satisfactions of *The Search For Meaning* is the letters I get which say: 'I'm amazed to find I have so much in common with the things people say on your program, which I would never have expected because we seem so different" . . . '

Caroline is intuitive in her work. She seems to know what it's like to be a woman at home. She is able to understand what it's like for the woman whose son was killed, who writes that she gets more comfort from *The Search for Meaning* than from her sessions with a therapist. She can feel what it is like to be an isolated old couple out there in the bush, who listen to their radio at the kitchen table and find themselves for the first time in their lives starting to talk with each other about matters of the soul.

Caroline knew that she was breaking a stereotype with a series of broadcasts from Aboriginal people, talking of their hopes and dreams, hurts, loves, and families. 'To hear black and white human beings describing their love and frailty— that's the revolution', Caroline said. 'It's the revolution of Jesus Christ. It's like yeast to the people where they wake up to each other, across the boundaries that have been deepened by denominations and politics. I don't care if the Phillip Adamses of this world think I've lost my punch as a journalist because I'm no longer getting stuck into people and sharpening my teeth on politicians. I'm not there to ask confronting questions. I'm there to listen, and to respectfully draw out the stories of Australian men and women. It's so clear. Thank you and goodnight'.

She winked, mocking herself. We were sitting in a little restaurant down by the harbour in her old stamping ground, where once she ran a sandwich bar. She's funny and quick, and she radiates in those moments like the flash of a wild pony's mane.

Caroline brings to the task of broadcasting a set of values that are not broadly obvious across the industry. They are values that seem anachronistic today; values that her segment of the Australian public respects; values that are part of her own refinement since 1981. Today she has a commitment to the way in which she uses, rather than pursues, controversy for controversy's sake. She is concerned to judge her performance in terms of whether or not it is achieving something worthwhile.

Caroline is endeavouring to take herself and her listeners to a more universal level of the human spirit. The program does not kick heads; it gives interviewees the opportunity to fill out a questionnaire beforehand, and then gives them the opportunity to delete what they don't like. Most broadcasters would laugh at the naïvety of that. Caroline's theory is that people will give more of themselves if they feel safe. Most people in the media would shy away from that level of vulnerability.

A commentator who would not be comfortable using Caroline's technique is Phillip Adams. He is not interested in sustaining that sort of intimacy, and thereby running the risk of exposing his own vulnerability. For Caroline, it is an almost unconscious practice to produce exactly the right atmosphere in which her subjects may open up.

Caroline's vulnerability, which is her strength and her weakness, it matched by a relentless professionalism, to the degree that we might ask, where is the woman, and where is the worker? She's professionally self-conscious, aware of herself and aware of the image she has. Conversely, she's not aware that people are looking at her when she walks into a restaurant.

In the recording studio with her producer Stephen Godley, Caroline slipped her spectacles into their tapestried pouch. She smiled at him across the controls. She slid a tan lipstick across her lips. Two young technicians, beyond the glass at another set of controls, smiled at Caroline. Everyone was attentive. Caroline looked realistic and earthy. She was confident, a little wild, wearing pants and shirt and only the lipstick for make-up. She introduced an Angry Anderson track. Stephen was encouraging her with his warmth, and Caroline was calm, exposed and yet still private in her performance. 'Lovely, Caroline', said Stephen. 'Good thing you've got a mind like a steel trap'.

'It's because I've got this piece of paper in front of me', she quipped.

She introduced a tape of Kath Walker, some readings from Julian of Norwich and the Gospel according to St Luke; she recommended a book called *If You Meet The Buddha On The Road, Kill Him!* by Sheldon Kopp. She whisked out of the room to get water for herself and her producer, loosening the belt that sat on her hips. This was informal but precise—including just the colleagues and not the guest.

'We call her one-take Jones', said Stephen, smiling.

We all listened quietly to Veronica Brady, a Catholic nun, who had been taped the day before. One of the young technicians brought Caroline and Stephen coffee. There was an old-fashioned pace.

Stephen and Caroline reaffirmed each other across the controls. There wasn't much ego in there. The emphasis was on producing well the content at hand.

'Have you got enough of it—it's about a minute-ten?'

Caroline shuffled her papers and picked up her glasses.

Her power rests in the two-way exchange of love between herself and her listeners. Her program, fuelled by this love and backed by her skill and experience, is one in which people consider her to be an expert. She is the first to say that she's not. She won't challenge people on issues because she knows that she's not intellectually equipped to do so. She has set herself up in the role of a religious figure with no theological training.

'I just can't feel that kind of passion anyway', said Caroline. 'The neutrality has become part of my nature. Don't forget I went to school in the ABC for the longest period and that creates a kind of neutrality'.

'There is some frustration for me in her even-handedness', said producer Stephen Godley, who is also an orthodox priest. 'Yet for Caroline to challenge would immediately make it someone else's program. Another presenter might have an expert sitting beside her, a trained priest or a theologian bringing specialist expertise.'

A theological scholar himself, and one who has lived within the Church, Stephen would be unable to resist challenging some of Caroline's guests if he were on the other side of the control box. 'I question my integrity still', he said, 'for not having leapt out of the control room at certain times when the frustration became too much for me. Caroline would be interviewing and I'd be tearing my hair out, with a voice screaming inside me to challenge the things that her guest would be saying'.

Caroline's critics would like her to interrupt: 'Hey wait a minute! That's fatuous! What do you mean by that?', instead of saying 'Oh, yes?' with an encouraging nod. Another criticism of her is that guests on the show are not interviewed by Caroline Jones: they interview themselves, and come up with all their own tired clichés. And another objection levelled at her is that some of the guests on her program have been frauds.

If Caroline's style of non-judgment is one that allows 'frauds' to reveal dimensions of spirituality in their personalities, dimensions that resonate with the listeners, then she is accomplishing her professional goal. Her commitment is to awaken people to their spiritual selves.

Her critics are reacting reflexively to the subject matter, and to her method. They attack her for doing something they don't consider worthwhile, for 'going off the deep end', and for having gone into an area that 'serious' people can't give credit to. None of this reflects on her nose for journalism and the fact that Caroline Jones is continuing to stimulate debate.

Caroline's critics expect her to establish a balance between cut'n'thrust challenge and story-telling. They will not find it so long as Caroline sits alone in the studio—she's not interested in developing it. 'I'm not big on choices, or on one thing cancelling out another', said Caroline. 'I'm quite happy to have contradictions sit there together. I like paradox. We're mad if we don't see problems as an opportunity to transform conflict, and its inherent negativity, towards a positive solution. Each crisis is a little death, and from death comes the resurrection.

'What I took to be destructive actions by some of the people in the ABC in relation to the program, actually gave me a push. It was a painful experience after putting years of love and energy into the program, with a huge audience response, to have the whole thing cut in half. It knocked me for a couple of months, and then I saw it a different way. I realised I didn't have to stay under the umbrella of the organisation. I could actually take my courage, my initiative and my own plans and be more independent. Why not take my own money and make a television series along the lines of *The Search For Meaning*?

'The motive came from the feelings of resentment and anger that I had towards those senior to me. Then I realised I needed to pray for them and myself. Suddenly, I had a whole new way of looking at the situation, which was, in fact, still exactly the same. My attitude had changed. Once again, I had come through the old "death and rebirth" metaphor. For me the symbol of death was my anger, resentment and arrogance, and then I had the grace (of God) to help me see that I didn't have to look at it that way any longer. The anger and resentment were transmuted into new energy to look at it creatively and independently. It felt like, once again, I could push myself beyond the chrysalis'.

For Caroline, the rhythm of life is now constantly measured by her awareness of 'after death comes a resurrection'. Her sense of well-being springs from her faith in God.

'There is also the feeling that suffuses me now that I will be cared for. I have faith in the love. I feel more powerful. It's not from a feeling of control, it's more a feeling of trust in what unfolds'.

Caroline's personal empowerment is still emerging. She is shifting from exerting the power of control to the realisation that who she is deserves to have what she wants. Her need to control was based on feelings of lack of self-worth and the effort to protect herself from loneliness and despair. It is now her self-love that is creating her sense of abundance.

She has found a spiritual path in the Church. She has a devil-may-care attitude towards her critics. Her sense of integrity, in her work, is intact. Communication, for Caroline, is the expression of her love.

'The dying and the ressurection is the centre of my meaning', she said quietly as she sat at her desk.

I had wandered down the silent, carpeted corridors, past the partitioned offices of ABC workers, to Caroline's office. The place was empty. The last colours of sunset were wrapping themselves around Centrepoint Tower. The skyline was backlit. Cars were weaving up William Street like a string of beads. Caroline was reading through some of her letters, feeling in company with her listeners. She is never alone when concentrating on her audience—she's suffused with love, admiration and gratitude with each daily mail delivery.

Caroline Jones, the servant of the public, is true to her dual commitment—to live her life in the grace of God, and to deepen the vocabulary of Australian discussion.

Jana Wendt

'NOW YOU'VE DONE EVERYTHING'

Jana Wendt grew up speaking Czechoslovakian at home and with her parents' friends. As a little girl in Melbourne she went off to school, and along with the other refugee kids, she struggled with English for the first time. She was the only child of cultured immigrants who doted on their dark-haired little daughter. Jana's Czechness is part of who she is. There are people in this country who would say 'get rid of the migrants'. Jana would set those people back on their heels.

She's a national treasure, courted by overseas networks, known throughout the land as Jana, often without the Wendt. Smart alecs say 'Oh—you mean Non-Event?', but that's just a nickname which confirms that she has won an important place in the heart of the nation. Few people have no opinion about her and everyone seems curious about what she's really like.

She's unique.

She's very slim. Tiny. Boyish.

She's funny. She laughs a lot.

She's super-intelligent. She is fluent in four languages. She swings between being utterly natural and revealing, and throwing a delicate, impenetrable web of protection around herself. It is hard to be offended, and easy to feel respect for the way she covers herself, and Brendan and Daniel, her husband and toddling son. They are the men in her life, the ones she loves. Jana is 33 and humming with the richness of her family life, which is paralleled by a television career matched by no other woman in Australia.

Gerald Stone, original producer of the 60 Minutes program, says of Jana: 'Of all the people who have passed through my hands she is designed for more sustained greatness. She has the potential for a bigger slice of stardom than any reporter I have dealt with. She's in Australia at the right time. She's the first Australian woman to take on the dominating role that Barbara Walters has in America. As an American, I found her particularly interesting. In the States, the cause for female rights and professionalism was further advanced than in Australia. Jana in her first days was given a very rough reception by females in Australian society.

'That proved what I had always been led to believe, that females are the worst and heaviest critics of other females. The country's initial reaction to Jana's being included in the 60 Minutes team was one of great hostility, in which we were seen as merely importing a bit of fluff to add glamour to the show.

'Jana's first 60 Minutes story was shot in Haiti—a hot, steamy place. In the final cut that went to air, she was seen wearing five or six different dresses. The piece was attacked not on the merits of the story, but at the nitpicking level of describing it as some sort of a fashion show. Of course, she had just worn a different dress each day because of the heat. The male reporters had changed their shirts without drawing the same attention.

'Of course', Gerald Stone continued, 'the upper end of the market, the more educated and career-oriented women, saw that if Jana succeeded there was more room for success'.

It is no accident that Australia is such a media-driven country, and that media barons like Rupert Murdoch originated here. There is a need for us to drag the world closer, to bring all other cultures here, just because they are so far away.

In Australia we have come to expect that if there is a major news event overseas—for example the San Francisco earthquake—Australian television stations will get footage from the overseas networks rather than having their own reporters on the spot. This isn't the case in the United States or England. They are still making an issue of satellite communication, because they are already able to enjoy their own and other countries' networks, which are all within range without the use of satellites.

Television is the cool medium, which insists that the way it's presented has to be thought through—pre-digested for the viewers. Radio, the hot medium, relies on raw reportage that generates images within the mind of the listener. Current affairs television is like a grown-up version of the old newsreels, where we'd dive off the street, and down some stairs into a darkened cinema where we'd become absorbed in the screen, maybe while eating lunch. The news would have been created weeks before, but we felt the excitement of seeing it for the first time on screen. It had been shot, processed, cut, and the soundtrack was synchronised with wonderful, stirring voice-overs that dared in those days to shape our thinking unashamedly: 'This is a just cause'; 'these men are evil'; 'we have implicit trust in our leaders'; 'foreign leaders, unless allies, are totally untrustworthy', and so on. We felt connected to the larger moments of the world, and judgments were being made in advance for us passively to accept. The news, presented as entertainment, was thrilling, compulsive viewing, as were

the cartoons and the shorts. Our attention spans shortened. We were being primed for television.

Now a current affairs program might present us with four or five stories in half an hour, on a network that's broadcasting up to twenty-four hours a day, every day of the year. We expect to be entertained while we are being informed, so our most successful presenters have mastered the art of selection and preparation of their reports. They hook us in, give us some basic facts, get some feelings flowing—compassion, anger, humour, disbelief—and wrap it up so that we are left with a few opinions about the topic, about the people involved in the topic, and not least, about the presenter.

It is said that a woman has to be either very clever or fairly stupid to make it in the television industry. Those perceived as stupid—the 'bimbos'—are hired to be all those things that men are prepared to allow them to be. They come from the Barbie Doll school of television presentation, with long legs and constant smiles. They are sexy in a vacuous sort of way, and often shrill of voice. They are frequently seen on morning television, all hairdo and lipstick, co-starring with a nuggety looking bloke who fits perfectly the macho mould required to balance whatever she is supposed to represent of womanhood.

The clever ones sidestep prejudice and judgment by displaying confidence in their own ability intelligently to present and analyse the material they are putting out to the viewer. They know how to downplay the tricky parts of their personalities, and come across as informed, assured and authoritative. They are likely to be nice to look at, though not necessarily classically 'pretty'; but their attractiveness lies more in the feeling that an evening spent with them would be stimulating, humorous, and informative.

Jana is like a stage actress, journalist and story-teller all rolled into one. Her interviewing style, her quirky glint, her use of her physical presence, have all been carefully focused to present a cool, allowing look. She has an edge to the tone of her voice: 'do anything, but don't bullshit'. She never babbles and she's not shrill.

Her craft as an interviewer is apparent. She sets up a sense of consistent stability in her interviews, offering the viewer an opportunity to reflect independently in order to formulate a personal response to the material. She demands much of her interviewees, but simultaneously gives the viewer breathing space.

A more demanding presenter would infuse her own personality into the experience. Just a smirk can slant a story, or a snicker; the inclusion of a well-chosen word can throw the viewers' personal world off-key, and bring them back to reacting to the presenter's personality.

Jana, among television women, is the most developed in her understanding of what works best for the medium. Her style is reminiscent of Swedish acresss Liv Ullman, who is distinguished by her perfectly crafted screen presence.

Jana is wary of baring too much of her soul or personality within the performance. She knows that if she strayed too far, for example while interviewing a politician, she would lay herself open to his seizing the unexpected intimacy to divert attention from the point of the interview—this notwithstanding the Dustin Hoffman and Robin Williams interviews, where her joie de vivre could not resist connection with theirs, and two magic television events were created.

To be so poised, Jana must suppress parts of her personality, parts that male interviewers can afford to open up. Richard Carleton, the original blood-on-the-hands interviewer, can allow himself the freedom to let go, dive out, and take a risk. He doesn't have to be liked; nor does Phillip Adams. They are allowed rough edges, which leaves them free to be self-deprecating without putting their credibility in jeopardy.

Jana measures the context in which she operates. She plays a role that makes her invulnerable, and she will survive. One reason for that is that she's likely to look wonderful for another twenty years!

The medium of television seems to attract sexy people. They survive in it because it's an environment that encourages a sexy, powerful feeling in people, and offers back its own form of sexiness. Those in the media business need a natural

JANA WENDT

sensuality. Dealing with human beings is an emotional business. It makes you laugh or cry, feel elated, sexy, depressed, joyous. It brings out all the emotions, and volatile people are attracted to it.

Some say that Jana is without peer. Her intelligence, timing and appearance are acceptable to both men and women. Like Delvene Delaney and Olivia Newton-John, she is one of the few women accepted by both sexes.

Jana chooses her own material. She limits what she does, not stretching beyond her known area of confidence and competence. She won't run a story unless she's certain to do it, and herself, justice. She has developed a touch of Mike Willesee's technique of tough, cold-blooded questioning, crafting her ability with indisputable intelligence. If there is a shortcoming to her interviews, it would be in the strict lines along which she operates, where she is not prepared to reveal the warmth of her personality and the depth of her knowledge: we get the Liv Ullman performance. It may be more exciting if her public repertoire included another performance, with a sense of abandon and improvisation, but Jana's at the top: there's a long way to fall, and she has to be circumspect.

Her success curve, dating from her beginnings as a newsreader on Channel 10, has been constant. Theories about how she has survived abound. Some say it's because in her early days she was not studio based: no one interfered with her development. She established herself in the freedom and creativity of *60 Minutes*, on the road, away from all the day-to-day backbiting and perceptions of what a 'studio girl' should be.

Many of us have become cynical about commercial television; yet before *60 Minutes*, many Australians were scarcely aware that there was a world beyond Australia. When we sent our own Australian reporters to faraway places, those places came to life. The format of *60 Minutes* is American, but it lends itself well to being Australianised.

Producer Gerald Stone unequivocally attributes Jana's success to her intelligence. Before she joined *60 Minutes*, he had seen tapes of Jana as a newsreader in Melbourne. 'She was too young then', he remembered, with a smile. 'She had the typical pudgy chin of a gorgeous-looking nubile young lady, but she was too fresh, too raw. I followed her for three years and then decided Wow! It's time we got her! She looked intelligent, striking, beautiful, with a tremendous potential, offset by what I would call a degree of university snobbishness; that style that seems to be bred in Australian universities, of people looking down their noses at anything that is mass market, or popular.

'But the success of that mass marketing', Gerald added, 'is to gauge what the psyche of the masses favours—what people really think about. For graduates like Jana there is still a protective attitude, that smacks of elitism'.

For Gerald, as producer, and Jana, as reporter, in the early days of *60 Minutes*, that 'protective attitude' became a stumbling block, because they had differing senses of news-value—a different feeling for what constituted a story. At that time, Jana's attitude towards a story that was crime-oriented, or one in which she herself took a high profile, was that she'd consider it too 'vulgar', according to Gerald Stone. As an intelligent and thoughtful person, Jana would have said that she was prepared to make some sacrifices for her work, but that there was a point beyond which she simply would not go; and she would be sincere in that.

It didn't mean that she wasn't prepared to stick her neck out. During her time with 60 *Minutes* she was often considered to be very abrasive—for a woman, of course. 'Jana had a notorious confrontation with an abortion doctor', Gerald Stone recalled. 'She was seen as hounding the doctor, from an anti-abortion stance, asking him questions that a lot of women resented. This enraged women who believed that she should have taken up the banner of their particular persuasion. It's a tremendous tribute to Jana that she was both able to overcome the wave of hostility, and weather the ongoing, second wave which meant that there are still feminists around who will not speak to Jana Wendt'.

Television is an industry that tests women. They knock their heads against the wall every day, one way or another. What has happened in the past ten years is that there has been a rush of young women into the industry, with a level of talent that some producers claim outstrips the young men of today.

'Ten-and-a-half years ago, when we first started', said Gerald Stone, 'ours would have been described as a typically sexist office—lots of jokes about girls, lots of flirting at Friday nights drinks sessions. The classic joke was that a pretty young researcher would come up and say "Here's my research", and the answer would be, "Never mind your research, show us your tits". That was standard, yet it was also like a kibbutz. The blokes were very protective of our women. They cared for each other.

'In these past years they have matured as a unit. As Gail Jarvis and Jana came in, they made the men feel like little boys going through the same tactics. So we started growing together. It's not as though we don't recognise the difference in the sexes. We all take pleasure when one of the women comes in with a new dress, or one of the guys has a new girlfriend'.

Well, that's television.

Fortunately for Jana, she met and married a man who understands and respects that she works hard. He doesn't find her weighty pay cheque emasculating. Jana and Brendan were married in 1984. 'It's nice to live comfortably—but I was living comfortably as a single man', Brendan said, stretching his arms to their full extent above his head, easing out of being questioned, only willing to speak with great reserve.

Brendan was a cameraman with the *60 Minutes* team. He was temporarily absent at the outset of Jana's time there: 'When she arrived at *60 Minutes*, I was off doing a feature film somewhere', he said. 'That was the start of 1982. I watched her a few times, and didn't think she was all that good. Then we were thrown together at the beginning of the following year. We did a couple of trips together and you just couldn't help liking her. She's a nice person, fun to be with, didn't stand on ceremony. She was great to live with'.

Like Jana, Brendan is an only child. Born in North Queensland, he's a nuggety, logical, no-nonsense, talented, independent Australian man.

'When you fall in love with someone, it just doesn't happen like that'. He looked at me mischievously, as though I would definitely need to have that explained. There was a hint of sarcasm in the way he had spoken. 'It happens over time, over a year. I fell in love with her because she is so refreshing. She has a healthy attitude towards life; a healthy injection of cynicism, plus joie de vivre. Every husband sees his wife as someone special—that's why he marries her. We were both anti-marriage, but then it happens and you think oh well, this is it, why stuff around?

'I've got no reason to reflect on this situation with Jana, no reason to analyse it. She's a top lady to work with. She's a well-adjusted human being, and they're hard to come by. Everyone sees her as a great intelligence. I don't see it that way; I see her basically as the woman that I love. If she was a university teacher, or a typist in a typing pool, she'd be the same person.

'I don't see her as a television star. She's a true professional, a good journalist, and she gets a buzz from doing good stories. 60 Minutes was the ultimate vehicle for her. She travelled the world, became a celebrity—and she was able to go off and do great stories. But it's a difficult job once you've decided to raise a child'.

Brendan says that nothing he will ever do will be as good after 60 Minutes. 'It was a one-off for both of us', he said. It was evening. Brendan had walked across the station lot to meet me in Jana's office. He was currently producing a program for the same network.

'Jana doesn't get carried away. Both of us are very cynical about this industry. I've been in it for 21 years and Jana—well, not as long. You have to accept the bullshit, understand that it is just that way—then you live accordingly. Part of the bullshit is doing women's magazine stories. Everyone complains that they never learn anything new about her, or see pictures of the baby. Well, they never will. I think people who don't keep their private lives to themselves get into a mess'.

Even though Brendan was answering me in sentences, it sounded as though he was speaking in monosyllables. He, like Jana, threw out an invisible defensive ring around his family.

'Her technique is evolving. "The perfumed steamroller" is one of the greatest misquotes of all time, because she hasn't always been that perfumed'. Brendan looked at me directly—a stranger—defying me to analyse that one.

Jana's office is a plain grey room with a high ceiling. A single little Wanda fish swims around in its cylindrical aquarium. The television tower strikes out into the sky through her window. There are no baby pictures, no Brendan pictures, no decorations, no plants. It's a plain, colour-co-ordinated work-room. The afternoon light brought out the flecks of grey in Jana's dark hair. Her long bones, slim arms and legs, were clad with absolute simplicity in a white T-shirt and well-cut linen pants. A Japanese roll cushion was behind her back.

On her desk was a big, well-worn diary and a proper nib pen. Stacked on the shelf behind her, next to a pile of videos, was *A Companion to Literature* and the Oxford Dictionary. Jana has long eyelashes, and minimal make-up on her Czech cheeks. She has tiny features, smooth skin, and quirky gold earrings. When she laughs in her office, it rings down the hallway. She had just weaned her baby boy.

'I feel like a journalist with an odd job', she said. 'I always thought that I'd like to be a journalist. The notion of talking about ideas was what interested me when I was young. I didn't have a quest, like eyeing the chair of Mike Willesee. I maintain an interest in things that I like.

'I've never been a directed person at searching out jobs. I've had a charmed existence in what I have done—lots of right places at the right time. I'm not one to push and shove— in fact, I'd rather not. I don't battle for a job. I'd battle for qualities or principles, even if I were working in the corner shop. But I don't like the idea of a ruthless battle to "get somewhere". At the same time, I can't imagine working in a pauper's situation in television because I've been so spoilt for so many years'.

The Nine Network, Jana's employer, was owned by the Bond Corporation: 'They invest in what they do. We have our skirmishes, but by comparison we're very lucky. If we said we wanted to shoot a run-up to the Presidential elections, we could just go and do it. There's definitely the consciousness of working in a medium that's in the forefront of change-over. We can see the speed and ease with which satellite is taking over our whole understanding of news. We think nothing of it. I'm so spoilt I don't know what it would be like to have to argue for anything.

'In my background, I didn't even get a whiff of discrimination, not even a hint of a feeling that someone might think that because you're a girl you should do such-and-such, and not the other. It was never part of my thinking that I was a girl and this is what girls do. I had no brother and sisters, and I was clearly raised believing that anything was possible.

'Part of that', Jana continued, 'has to do with the cultural background of my parents. They came from a country where there was no suggestion of that. There are many cultures and nationalities where the rigid division between male and female roles is a severe problem. It just so happens that Czechoslovakia is the opposite'.

We talked about Milan Kundera's *The Unbearable Lightness of Being*, and how the movie of the book contrasted the eccentric free-spiritedness of the Prague women with the austerity and tradition of women from Geneva. 'Czechoslovakia was regarded as the democratic heart of Europe, before things started to go dramatically wrong, starting with Adolf', Jana said. 'It was an open and sophisticated place. From my background has come the disbelief that there is an attitude of restriction for women. My background says that a woman can do exactly what she wants to do'.

Jana was resting her elbows on her desk. Her delicate fingers were interlocked, with pale pink fingernails glistening like shells. Her wedding ring is a flat, rectangular piece of black onyx with a large diamond set in the middle—an heirloom from Brendan's family. It reminded me of Jana's description of herself ('I'm an island, you know') when I had first approached her for an interview. She takes pride in the enigmatic quality of being self-contained.

'It's hard for me to avoid feelings of sympathy for refugees, having had a refugee beginning myself. I've seen on my own skin what a refugee lifestyle is like; what it means for people to have to uproot and leave something they love very much. It touches me personally when I hear of people from places like Vietnam, who find themselves in tin-pot boats for days or months, landing on foreign soil and in some unlucky cases, getting slapped in the face and told to get back in their boat and sail off.

'I've learned to understand the hankering refugees have for the sweet element of life that they had, and don't have any more. I sympathise deeply with that. It's what I know, too, and what I've grown up with. Some people really don't understand the refugee pain. They think the "reffos" are bloody lucky to be here. Of course they're lucky to be here. On the other hand, some migrants want too much, they expect it too soon, and they want Utopia tomorrow.

'I know that all a refugee has is a memory, because they have had to shed all the tangible things that we value in life—not necessarily property, but places that they love, hearing the language spoken in the streets that they loved. Refugees talk about those sorts of things to people they are close to. My parents were not people to burden outsiders with their memories, but they talk to me and to some who are close to them.'

It's no wonder Jana has won so many hearts. There is such a waif-like quality to her physical presence that she makes you think of the archetypal fairy-tale child, who should have been a princess in her own land but who finds herself transported to a different place, lacking the grace and style in which she should rightfully have been immersed. Yet even under inauspicious circumstances, she finds a way to shine, her natural breeding illuminating her path as she steps lightly towards fame, fortune, love and happiness.

She has a deep love of music, inherited from her father. Music in her family is one of the ways by which they are able to transport themselves back to their other world. Her father's favourite composer is Janacek, and Jana, too, has an extensive collection of some of his most obscure pieces. For music to soar through her baronial, yet cosy, home, is for her to be filled with the essence of her European roots.

Right now, Jana was preparing for an interview with Russ Hinze, who was being hauled over the coals of Queensland for alleged huge illegal loans. She was reading, and marking each piece of photocopied material in readiness. One of her *A Current Affair* researchers came in, offering embellishments to the script. He was there to tutor her on the nuts and bolts of the interview. Jana, who often blushes, blushed.

'I want to generalise it a bit more—find out how embarrassable he is', she said.

'We can ask him about the signature his wife gave in her maiden name', the researcher offered.

' "You've been in politics for ten or fifteen years and you're telling me you can't understand what your accountant said?" ' practised Jana. Suddenly, she was on track, confident of the organisational skills behind her.

Her researcher sat quietly on the bench behind her chair, smoking, listening, thinking, giving her ideas for questions, filling her in. At that moment Jana was like a secretary, taking notes from him as he went through the information. They were both trying to figure out the details of Hinze's doings, commenting that they could not believe that Hinze would follow through with the interview arrangements.

'Can you make him cry?' asked the researcher. They both chuckled as he left the room. Jana continued to write details, quickly. The phone might ring at any time now; Hinze would be leaving the courtroom. When he does, Jana will race over to make-up, and on to the studio to link up with him. She glanced at her black-faced watch, a match for her wedding ring.

'Yes, Ross', she answered into the phone. 'What's been dumped on him today? Oh, ah, uh. Oh, so there's no end to this? D'you reckon he's not going to do it? Should I dismiss it from my mind altogether, or pretend it's going to happen? All right, thanks mate'.

She put her feet up on a side desk, and patted her thigh.

'Big Russ got more shit dumped on him today'. I felt like a shadow figure that responds.

Another researcher brought in some fax sheets, still warm, from Brisbane.

'I'm shocked and horrified', said Jana as she read some of the court proceedings. She stayed calm, having decided to keep taking notes as though he would still come on air. That's her professionalism; she's positive, she makes sure everyone still feels confident and capable by her determination to be absolutely polished and ready for Hinze, even though the interview might not happen.

She sat with a scrunched-up chin in her hands, reading; she took another phone call, and pulled her earring off absent-mindedly.

Her irritability was rising. It's all very well to have the material supplied and for her researcher's point of view to be heard. 'But then', she said, 'I want to distil it according to my own code. At that point I want to be left alone so I can get in touch with my own attitude, organise my questions. This isn't a pretty story, but it's a great example of the line between black and white. My style is to go after such a person, because I know there are hundreds of thousands of people out there who'd like to speak to Russ Hinze tonight.

'Usually I do this stuff at home in the mornings, but there wasn't enough material until this late in the day. I'm the chickie in the chair, so I have to make it work for me. After that, I can let myself out of my room, and prowl'.

Jana was displaying just a hint of being highly strung; it was a relief to experience the chink in her perfection, within the spirit of her independence. No one working like she does could maintain a super cool indefinitely. Once she shuts the door, that the sign that she's rolling.

Five nights a week she's on. Five days whose mornings are spent at home, with phones and faxes to give her an idea of what's coming up once the real work starts for her at around midday, when she leaves home to go to work. *A Current Affair* goes to air on Channel Nine after the evening's *National News*. It's networked to country stations later in the night. Five million people scrutinise Jana every weeknight. Not a single detail escapes them.

'I don't make a conscious effort to hide anything—but I have a kind of sense of how to present myself to people I don't know, whose living rooms I occupy every night', Jana said. 'I don't regard television as this terrible pernicious element in our culture. Certainly, the tendency to use it as an anaesthetic is tragic. By rights it should open up people's minds rather than closing them down—after all, it's presenting a whole wide world to you instead of just a narrow slice of it. But it does seem to serve the tendency in human nature towards laziness.

'I look at my performance in the same way as meeting people for the first time. There is a certain way that I would behave, and that's probably the way I've decided to present myself on air. I can't imagine having the sort of conversation I am having with you now at 6.30 p.m. in front of a television camera, because it would not be appropriate. I pop up after a news service, with the hope of offering more information on newsy subjects. I don't think it would be appropriate for me to do the odd one-liner in the middle of all that'.

Jana would not be comfortable being any more revealing on camera than she is. The Czech girl, the Australian woman, has an element of formality tucked away in her genetic make-up. As we mulled this over, Jana put her legs up on a chair opposite our sofa.

'Well, I don't know if it's a Czech trait. We are already cheeky enough as journalists in Australia, without having that extra incursion of "Not only do I want you to tell me everything but I'm going to be as familiar with you as I can—Well, Fred, blah, blah . . . " Not "Hullo, Mr Smith, let's have a talk!" Maybe it's Czech. I know it's old-fashioned, pretty conservative. There's a line there for me, a cut-off point. A bit of me is fairly eccentric and noisy, and a bit of me is this more austere-seeming person.

'When I'm familiar, like with Brendan and family friends—that's the playful side. When I'm on camera, I don't want to presume too much. Australians have a habit of being much more familiar than me. I like that! All over Europe there is greater formality. Maybe there is something ethnic in me'.

I had attempted to hypothesise to Jana that her austerity, her screen-star beauty, and her precision, could be likened to that of Liv Ullman; a Liv Ullman with a middle European background.

She laughed. 'Oh, then John would be Ingmar Bergman?'

John Westacott, executive producer of *A Current Affair*, is an orderly looking man, trim of beard, twinkling of smile. He was laughing. 'Liv Ullman and Bergman work out a fantasy in a movie which has a beginning and an end', he said. '*A Current Affair* deals with real emotions, real happenings, day in and day out. We are reacting to that. We can't sit down and craft two hours of fantasy. Liv has that implacable, detached, beautied perfection in her performance. Jana has the consistency that is extraordinary'.

John was in his office. His team moved around the big office beyond the glass partition.

'It's her program, her emotion, her thoughts', he continued, 'and not only is she good enough to present like she does every night, but she's also good enough to put and keep an intelligent, fast-thinking team behind her. It's a bit like a fantastic steam train. The engine—Jana—must be strong enough to drag the whole train along. It's intermeshed'. He swung his chair back. It was the eleventh hour, just before on-air time, and his enthusiasm kept rolling. 'It's the most amazing thing with her, it's a helluva thing', he said. 'The set of emotions and interactions all being fronted every night by one person, and there is no other perception wanted or needed other than Jana's.

'Is the boiler back?' he called out referring to Jana in the term Reg Ansett once applied to his air hostesses. 'She's an amazing person. There is tension, but it's inside, and she handles it with a deep equanimity. She has an interesting reserve, and a certain poise in her professional and personal life that doesn't seem to break down under stress. Everyone pushes information at her, and she has to sort it all out, trust the people who are feeding her, and then turn her mind to a sensible interview'.

John Westacott produced Mike Willesee for his last six months, and then made the transition to Jana. 'Willesee had perception, and timing, and absolute nerve', John said. 'There's a story about a challenge he put out to one of his interviewees, who was reputed to be a cheat. "No, I'm not", was the guest's reply. "Well show me your licence", Willesee ordered. "It's in the car", the bloke said. "Well, go and get it", commanded Willesee.

'Well, you know, on national television, that takes some nerve, because all the bloke had to do was to pull it out. The story is that Willesee was tipped off beforehand that the bloke wasn't carrying a licence. Very brave, and great timing. Michael was 46 then. Jana is 33 and every bit as good. She's everything she wants to be'.

He smiled, and leaned forward. 'I may be regarded as being slightly sexist; there were no more accommodations for Jana than there ever were for Willesee, other than that she had a child and needed to breast-feed. I'd tear my hair, and then I realised that I had to make the necessary mental adjustment to fit that into the day. It lasted not much longer than six months, so there was that daily extra little strain—very, very minor!'

Jana and I were climbing the stairs back to her office one mid-afternoon. I was aware of Jana, the mother, stepping out in front of me.

'Do you get homesick at work?' I asked.

She turned around and faced me squarely. 'Yes, very. It's really quite painful'.

Jana's work-day peaks at the home/child 'witching hour'. At that time of day she is likely to be found in 'make-up', knowing that the nanny, in her stead, is caring for Daniel. She might be bathing him, having a cuddle, making his tea, watching him bang around the kitchen, reading him his story, settling him down.

'It's not something that I even reveal in an office like this', said Jana. 'It's not the focus of most people's day, who I work with. I can't spend hours impressing on people that I'm missing my son, and it's really trying. I do know that having a baby was the most wonderful thing to have done. It would have been very sad if I had not had him. I would lack a dimension that's well worth having, for the work that I do. I haven't had a son so that I get an extra dimension to my work, but the spin-off does give it depth'.

Jana is sure of what it is in life that matters to her. She has values and refined parts of her life that she doesn't need to associate with her performance: they are her love of music, and her quieter, laid-back side.

As Brendan said: 'Most weekends we don't see anyone, other than each other and our baby. After a week of being in the spin dryer of daily television we're more than happy to come home and just talk to each other, or read the paper, go for walks, and play with the baby. We like good classical music, we both enjoy food and wine and each other's company—and we have a similar attitude towards privacy'.

Some media people try too hard. It's their nature. The hunger is there all the time. It doesn't matter how much they get fed, the hunger is still there. They have an appetite for the energy and the movement, and having something to say. They'll even take time out to tip who's going to win the Rugby League. Jana is able to lean back from it and say: 'There are parts that are just not worth it . . . ' It's obvious that Jana at least takes time to refuel herself.

'I don't do anything extra for my health', she said. 'I run around after my son. I eat well, and lots. I've always been a self-taught yoga person and I'm just coming back to that because I think it's terrific. To me it's a peace-making process. I don't meditate and I'm not up on the spiritual elements of yoga, though I know they're important. I just like the physical extension of it'.

Feeling personally powerful is an insurance against being exploited. Part of Jana's personal power is that she has created a family life for herself which restores her, and offers her a comparatively soft option at the end of the day and the week. She knows that she is not depending on her work for emotional satisfaction. She has a supportive partner who can assist her to reflect on her working life from a little distance.

Will she stick at it? A fantasy hovers in the back of their minds for Jana and Brendan, of being somewhere in the Italian countryside eating bread and olives, studying art, and visiting places of beauty.

In the years to come, if she does continue, Jana will certainly be one of the highest-paid people in the history of Australian television. She and her family will have access to constant and great wealth. Recently Jana was courted by a United States network who wanted to woo her over to America. Even the initial fee amounted to millions. It would have involved compromise, of course, beyond the obvious loss of her job with *A Current Affair*, and the interruption of her family stability. Would she be more empowered if she stayed at home, protecting her privacy, staying within known boundaries, enjoying the local adulation of her skill and beauty? If she accepted the American deal, would she be giving away personal power in exchange for the power of money, and the seduction of having the collective consciousness of as many as two hundred million people directed towards her?

If Jana decided to work in a larger setting, she would have to believe in her own ability to be as important in that setting, and as powerful, as she is here. She could legitimately assume that she would be. The hardest thing for someone in her position would be not to believe her own public relations story. If she went to America she would have a huge and capable PR machine behind her, promoting her as the darling of Australia, the sharpest and most beautiful journalist, the most intelligent and hard-hitting personality. There would be dynamic film clips to prove it, and music, glamour, and pizazz.

In the face of all that, regaining her own centre and sense of identity, and a sense of what is manageable in her life, would be immensely challenging for both Jana and Brendan. The job could be an irresistible force that drove them in its path away from the other things they had dreamed of, such as having another child, or studying in Florence, or climbing a steep hill to a farmhouse at weekends. She would have to muster enormous belief in herself to put the Jana that we see on our TV screens on to American screens. Her ego would have to perform at its maximum, never letting up.

Weeks had passed. Jana was relaxing in her office. She had turned down the United States offer. 'I think in my area of work, often there are things that outsiders view as enormously powerful', Jana said. 'Possibilities and options, that I regard as the exact opposite. While obviously if I were to consider signing a big contract for the United States, in objective terms it would be a powerful position to hold, at the same time there would be an element of disempowerment in there for me too. I might gain something. But I might lose the most important part of myself, and my life, and the things that I consider to be important'.

'Jana, how would you describe that in terms of the American contract requiring too much ego, and involving the loss of your alignment between your ego and your soul?'

'You're talking about having that absolute internal balance', said Jana, 'and that's not easy. We all play games with other people, and we also play games with ourselves. We conceal things from ourselves, efficiently and effectively. You can go through a lifetime concealing truths from yourself. It's not until you confront certain areas of your life that the chasm between what's true and what is your own invention becomes obvious. Certainly this job that I do is conducive to forgetting about any inadequacies that I might have'.

'Does Brendan serve as a conscience for you?'

'He does. I would hope that to a degree I can do that now, on my own. But then, that might be the masterful act of kidding myself. I am very aware of that. In fact, I become more, rather than less, aware of it as I go along. I think I've passed the peak of thinking that everything was perfect some monumental aeon ago! I don't know whether that has something to do with getting older, or having more experience in this field. I monitor myself, to make sure that there is an approximation between reality and my own beliefs about myself.

'The television game is certainly conducive to developing self-admiration skills—the ego, if you like. You could sit back and say "I am a marvellous human being with absolutely infinite talents"—which necessarily is nonsense. The trouble is that people sometimes believe it of themselves. Television is a dangerous area.

'It takes a long time to get through to the honest core of yourself. In our honest moments we can reflect, and think about our weaknesses. I now do that honestly. I think once the door is cracked open there is no choice. I don't think the crack can be pasted over; once we've had a glimpse, we can't decide that we won't think about it any more.

'Fulfilment in here, at work? No, I'd never say fulfilment. There is satisfaction, sometimes great satisfaction. Fulfilment for me is to do with being at home, definitely, most definitely. To be honest, my ego does get away from me in here. I'm certainly conscious of when ego is there as a force, and when I'm exerting it'.

'What would happen if you pulled back from ego and tried to be more as you are at home, when you're in here—dealing primarily in the power of love?'

'Vulnerability. The vulnerability that I'd expose myself to if I did do it, would be enough to make any reasonably professional woman not do it. If you're smart enough in the workplace, you have mechanisms to protect you from too much pain. There's extension of all those feelings in the vulnerability of home. It must be very hard for people for whom there's no home to expose that vulnerability—and soul, if you like.

'But to contradict my own argument, it depends on how much time you spend with people in the workplace. The barriers and restraints and protections that you allow yourself to build up, will get whittled away over time as trust develops. I don't think it's safe to operate in that defenceless, barrierless way, every day of my working life; and without home and love, there would be no balance for the soul'.

How defended Jana would have needed to be to take on America! How much ego would have been involved? How little soul? It would have been disempowering for her, in terms of the truth of being herself.

To which Jana added: 'Until you get detachment from the picture, and can say to yourself that this is no more than a potential blaze of glory. It's when I retreat from it that I can actually see more clearly what is actually important for me'.

'Do you think it's hard for some women to have the fulfilment and softness without the loving?'

'Yes, I think that would be enormously hard. Enormously, because I think you would feel like half a person, or a fraction of a person. The home fulfilment is a terribly basic, right-feeling fulfilment. It feels as though you should have done it a long time ago, and this is the way you actually should be. I think I'm pretty lucky. I remember something my father said to me, when I had literally just had Daniel. I rang him up and said: "Hello, I've just had a son," and he said: "Well, now you've done everything, you've really done everything!"

'I think that's right. I don't mean "everything" like stood on top of the Eiffel Tower, but I've done it so that I can understand that alignment—what you call the alignment of the ego and the soul, leading to the power of love. I don't think you can know this until you feel it. I don't think you can have a grip on it, although you can have an intuition about it.

'It's crucial to reflect on the spiritual component of oneself. My instinct has a lot to do with my family, and my parents' family. My father, particularly, was keen to talk about what he would regard as real values, so that I was conscious of the concept that there are real values that have to be preserved, that are best preserved if you want to be a complete human being. Not that it was ever enunciated like that, but there was the strong feeling that values were more important than superficiality and appearances.

'I do sometimes think that some women I know in high-powered jobs have lost track of the spiritual component completely. I would like to think that it's there somewhere, but often it's bloody hard to find. You can't really appreciate something that you've never reached out for. So you can't expect them to appreciate the spiritual component, for instance, if they've never reached out for it. I think it's sad if they've never tried to find something other than the level of the daily work life.

'It's to do with love. I know a lot of people have recoiled, after being near-mortally wounded in their effort to find love'.

For all her strict professionalism and her immaculate way of presenting herself, the thing that is essentially captivating about Jana is the mischievous quality of her love. When Colin Beard and I arrived at her place on the morning we had arranged to take photographs of her, it felt as though everyone had gone somewhere else. We knocked at the wrong door.

There was movement inside. Jana was signalling us as she moved across the space inside to the real front door. We had to go around the corner of the building, and by then she was in the garden with her welcoming, irrepressible, fully attentive, smiling self. We hadn't seen each other for some time. Jana was warm and bubbling. Colin, very laid-back, was intent on aiming for the truth with his camera.

The three of us moved into the kitchen, catching up on news. Jana made a good strong brew of coffee, and Colin wanted to talk about clothes. He had a fantasy of photographing Jana as a European maiden in a summer dress, looking something like Elvira Madigan. Jana doesn't have any Elvira Madigan clothes in her wardrobe. She's graceful and essentially tailored.

There was a high chair in the kitchen, and absolute order. Her fridge is like everyone's fridges, with bits of this and that, reminders and memorabilia stuck to its door. There were photographs of the love she has surrounded herself with, one of her round little cherub son, who will grow up to be bilingual. There was another of three ethnic women smiling modestly at the camera, in black dresses and black scarves, symbolic of Jana's roots.

Jana's choice of music mingled with the toys, the paintings and the baby blankets. The music of Leos Janacek reflects elements in Jana's nature. His operas, composed around conflict, reveal an intellectual discourse between the instruments and echo Jana's intensity, intellectuality, clarity and passion.

I turned to wave to Jana as we drove away. She was like a freeze frame, with her dark hair, and plain black pants and top, standing on the balcony against the backdrop of the secure, understated white residence that is her home.